IS COMMUNISM
DEAD FOREVER?

James K. McCollum

University Press of America,® Inc.
Lanham • New York • Oxford

Copyright © 1998
University Press of America,® Inc.
4720 Boston Way
Lanham, Maryland 20706

12 Hid's Copse Rd.
Cumnor Hill, Oxford OX2 9JJ

Library of Congress Cataloging-in-Publication Data

McCollum, James K.
Is communism dead forever? / James K. McCollum.
p.   cm..
Includes bibliographical references.
1. Communism—Romania. 2. Romania—Politics and
government—20th century. 3. Post—communism—Romania.   I.
Title.
HX373.5.M38 1998   335.43'09498—dc21   98-39211 CIP

ISBN 0-7618-1259-8 (cloth: alk. ppr.)
ISBN 0-7618-1260-1 (pbk: alk. ppr.)

Contents

FOREWORD

It was a real pleasure to me to read Professor McCollum's new book about Romania and other former communist countries, written after such a long experience in this country, initially as a Fulbright fellow and then as a professor at different universities and the motor of the program, "Interns from Romania at UAH." By having so many friends in Romania in different social media and by visiting different units, he had the opportunity to know directly the real problems of the Romanian society and economy. Therefore, I think such a book is more credible for a foreigner than one written by a Romanian, who always can be suspected of *partie pris*, as well as by a foreigner with a shortage of live documentation, by sharing some time with the Romanians as a friend and as a social and economic observer.

I also like the way he chose to present the situation as a case story which makes the reading more interesting, attractive, and credible. But, of course, he did not live here for decades to feel more completely the atmosphere and the cultural action of brain-washing, in different directions and by using different "detergents," the main being the fear concerning your present and future, as well as the life and the future of your children and your family.

This climate determined the opportunism to become a real state religion and it was and still is exploited successfully by the power, because the morality and the mentality are not changing as fast as the rules of the economic game. Therefore, even when, or if, these new rules are formulated, they are not really respected and the reform is going on slowly and with difficulties.

On the other hand, you must take into account that the Romanian society between the two world wars was far from perfect. There were great discrepancies between the social classes, especially between the peasants and the poor people living in the big cities and the very rich people, few of them spending fortunes abroad or in the country for very unproductive purposes.

Romania, being at the intersection of important commercial ways, was attractive for the powerful empires: Turkish, Russian, and Austrian and therefore the rulers were almost always influenced by these empires, in times when Romanian *pricipates* were not occupied by these powers. Therefore, you find a greater influence of the western civilization in Transilvania, which was under the Austrian-Hungarian empire for a long time, ruled in a more ordered and bureaucratic way, as well as under the influence of the Catholic and Reformed churches, than in Moldavia and Muntenia where the Russian and Turkish influence is more powerful and the Orthodox church is dominant. It is well known that there are some differences in the practice and the cathechism of the two sister churches, but these differences induced in time big differences in the behavior of the inhabitants. There is a Romanian saying, "Do what the priest says, not what he is doing." In spite of the fact that the history imprinted genetically the cultural behavior in some measure, the European cultural influence developed a new mentality especially after the 1948 revolution and after the Union of the Romanian Principates, in 1959, with some French assistance and mainly after Carol I came as a ruler of the Unified Principates.

The gaining of the declaration of independence after the Russian-Romanian-Turkish war, in 1878, and the proclamation of the Romanian Kingdom, the position of Romania in Europe strengthened and the development of the new class of industrialists started. This development was amplified after the First World War when Transilvania, Bessarabia, and Bucovina joined the Old Romanian Kingdom and formed the "Great Romania." The economic power of Transilvania and Banat influenced in a great measure, the economic situation of Romania. Its currency was very strong and Romania offered a great amount of cereals, meat, timber, salt, and oil for export.

In the same time, Romanian industry developed rapidly in some directions by the efforts of clever men like Malaxa in metallurgical and machine building industries (locomotives and tanks mainly), oil industry developed in the Prahova valley, and some electrical industry. The German influence along with American (Ford in Bucharest, oil companies in the Prahova valley, and the telephone network and communications) became more and more important. The promises for a modern industrial development in Romania were. The Soviet occupation and the forced abdication of King Mihai I and the communist regime changed from the roots the rules of the economic and social game. Communism represented for many people a good promise and hope, but unfortunately revolutions are brutal and many people suffered because of this brutality in prisons and at the Danube-Black Sea Channel (first version). The middle class, which did exist at that time - and the family in the case presented belonged to it - suffered a lot and this was a great mistake and the main point in breaking up the democracy. The so called "popular democracy" was in fact the dictatorship of a non-civilized and brutal group in the name of the proletariat, by copying the Soviet example.

After the death of Stalin, the situation did not change essentially; the main achievement being the so called "Declaration of Independence from the Soviet Union" and the withdrawal of Soviet army units from Romania in 1964. Very soon, after the death of Gheorghiu-Dej, the communist ruler of Romania in 1965, and the coming to power of Ceausescu, the way for national communism was open. The forced industrialization started producing great social and economic changes, some of them good (the economic power increased and an industrial civilization developed at a fast pace), some of them bad (especially concerning the environment and the development of the underculture). The industries were developed in a high pace (there was considered a Romanian miracle), but in an inefficient way, as proved to be on a long term, because of a managerial crisis and great changes concerning the markets after 1989 (COMECON) disappeared and new markets could not be found in a short time).

But some achievements cannot be denied, such as the Danube-Black Sea Channel, the underground metropolitan in Bucuresti, some electrical power centrals - built mainly by the internal forces of the Romanian economy.

This way was combined with a hyperbolic cult of personality (which was a characteristic of totalitarian regimes not just in Romania and not born in Romania) of the president and of his wife, which ended by their pharonic behavior and the complete loss of dignity of the population in relation to the power until December, 1989 (with only two exceptions: Lupeni, 1977 and Brasov, 1987). It is not easy to replace this behavior, determined by the permanent risk of being suspected by the omnipresent Securitate, by a correct and civilized behavior characteristic to a real democracy. This can be an explanation of the slow going reform of the presidency of Mr. Iliescu as well as the way in which his party, the PDSR, understood how to rule the country. This period of time represented a change to the better by comparison with Ceausescu's time and created promises for a real democracy, more complete and compatible with the European Union democratic regime.

The too-long transition time under PDSR (*Partie Democratic Social Reform*, the political party of Ion Iliescu which emerged from the National Salvation Front) rule created an unfair distribution of the national wealth by abuse and breaking of the laws because of the low level of political and economic culture of the people. In the same time, the efficiency in using the real economic potential of Romania decreased dramatically. The privatization was slowly moved on, being accelerated after the 1996 elections by the government under Victor Ciorbea. But it is self understood that without this phase, too long and with low efficiency for the nation, the change represented by the elections of 1996 could not be possible. It started a new period, full of hope for betterment, but unfortunately not yet achieved in the results of one year of democratic government.

Unfortunately, 'till now none of the post-revolutionary governments succeeded to valorify (put in good account) the great potential of the agriculture, tourism, and some industry and to diminish the corruption and Mafia-like economic behavior in the economy and society. The SME (small and medium enterprises) which emerged in great numbers after the revolution, are now in a difficult situation - suffocated by the lack of funds and by the bureaucracy, as well as by hard conditions of an economy in crisis (the media reports that 2/3 of them are either bankrupt or terminated for other reasons.

Romanians still hope for betterment and accept the sacrifices to quickly bring normal times of life which the country's resources and the people's hard work should bring. Now is the time to mention the very low level of salaries and the high level of prices which are almost at the same level as in the western countries. Part of the difficulty results from low productivity, lack of motivation of the work force, a managerial crisis, a shortage of professionals, and generally low morale. This correlation is very unfavorable for the Romanian society which doesn't have the same capacity to accept the difficulties and dedication to work hard as the Germans and Japanese after the second world war in spite of a rather high degree of intelligence and problem solving capacity. They need material motivation after such a long time of privation of the last decade of the communist era.

Intellectuals and property renters are especially in difficult circumstances because of low levels of salaries and pensions as well as a shortage of jobs in their professions. Real hope is felt only by some of the young technicians (some computer engineers and economists). There is a real need for courage and initiative to start a new business, but some people have these qualities and have been very successful with new businesses. However, there is a real danger in case the Reform will not be successful in 1998, that social events will compromise the whole process of democratization and economic reform and bring to power national extremists or another kind of dictatorship. One pattern that is possible is that often seen in South America. This pattern must be avoided. Doing so is mainly the responsibility of the Romanians, but good assistance programs from the USA and EU will be very helpful in cultivating real democracy in all aspects of economic and social life (civil society, justice, government, mass media, etc.) to stop the Mafia-like behavior in different sectors and to impose respect for the laws.

There is real hope that the new generation will be able to replace the feudal-like and Mafia-like behavior with real democratic and civilised behavior in respect of the laws and of common sense (which must be reeducated in the spirit of humanism and respect of the other's opinions if they are not harmful for the society or the community). This will take time and unfortunately there is not yet a perfect society to be taken as a model - even the American society has some undesirable aspects, as we can see in the American movies (violence, drugs, prostitution, crime, a.s.o.)

As is well known, we cannot look to the future by neglecting the past. Therefore, we must take all good things from the past, even from the communist experience, and try to build a future based on promises of modern society determined by the high level of technology, including information technology and communications.

Unfortunately, after the revolution, the educational system declined, perhaps only temporarily, but the number of illiterates increased and the interest in good education decreased in favor of making money. Making money became a scope in itself and a new class of newly enriched people, like the war enriched, was born after the big change in 1990. This class is formed mainly by former security officers and Communist party activists as well as by people who illustrated themselves by breaking the laws and stealing money and goods from the rest of the population. The Caritas and Safi (pyramid schemes) examples, as well as the cases of some banks such as DACIA FELIX and COLUMNA are well known. We are still waiting for the guilty to be punished and justice rendered.

Therefore, I consider that a long way must still be covered to reach a democratic society based on justice and truth and the title of this book is completely justified. The communism as we knew it is dead forever, but some new forms of extremism can appear. If Christianity, after 2000 years, still has a lot of difficulties and failures, we understand that to build a better society is not at all an easy historical task and our life time is too short to hope to see it at work. But let us try to contribute to this construction.

I am convinced that this book, like all of Dr. McCollum's activity in Romania, is devoted to this great task. I think that the book can be useful to anyone wanting to better understand the Romanian society. It contains a story written by a hand that was moved by an American eye and brain, but should help readers from all cultures to understand our plight.

Is Communism Dead Forever?

Preface

The challenge to participate in the transition of a former communist country into democracy and free market conditions seemed daunting, yet extremely interesting. For too long, we had looked at the peoples across the former iron curtain as enemies and we preferred that they be strong democrats and allies. When I was selected to be a Fulbright Scholar to go to Romania in 1991, my wife and I were very excited to learn what communism had wrought on a country in the more than forty years of its existence and to see what we could do to assist in the transition to democratic conditions. We had few illusions that we could make a strong impact on the country in the ten (later to be extended to eleven) month assignment, yet we wanted to see what was possible. During the eleven months we worked in Romania with visits to all of the other Eastern European countries except Albania and the former Yugoslavia we felt that we had made some impression on the Romanians although much more needed to be done.

In numerous additional returns to Romania, including one program that allowed me to bring 53 Romanians to America for business internships, we have found that the situation was worse than we realized in September, 1992, when we returned to the University of Alabama in Huntsville. The old habits and mentality established under the communist system have impeded the movement toward democracy and free market much more than we thought possible. This has been the situation in all of the former communist countries. Communism has had a deep effect on the unfortunate citizens who have experienced it. We pilgrims from western countries found it difficult to understand that many people who have lived under communism do not think as we think and do not react as we react in both political and economic situations, but it is true for many of them.

I have searched the 'post-communist' literature and found mostly in former communist countries are the writers saying that the transition is going to be long and difficult. Because of this, I felt that I had a duty to tell the democratic world of the continuing effects of communism even though the system has been discredited. Communism still rules the lives of almost two billion people even today and still affects the lives of millions more. We need to examine the phenomenon in all of its aspects and learn from the unfortunate experience to better appreciate our own system and to renew our determination to prevent such a system as communism from spreading in the future.

I thought it would be useful to examine life under the communist system by presenting the pattern of one person's life in a case study. Additionally, we have used information gathered from hundreds of meetings and interviews with other people: managers, educators, farmers, and workers who toiled under the communist system. The impressions we gathered show that progress is being made, but not at the rate most of us feel is possible and many inequities are occurring on the road to democracy and free market. We hope that the ideas presented here will lead to improved decisions within former communist countries and better assistance programs from western countries.

Romania and all of the former communist countries of Eastern Europe want to join the European Union (EU) and NATO. Poland, the Czech Republic, and Hungary were accepted for membership in these organization s in mid-1997. Several other former communist countries were accepted for EU membership in late 1997, but many others, including Romania, were rejected. At the same time, it appears that western support has shifted to a primary focus on Russia in 1997-1998, and the other former communist nations are less favored.

I want to express great appreciation for the recommendations I have gotten concerning this effort. Dr. Niles Schoening and Dr. Dianna Bell of UAH have read the entire manuscript and made valuable suggestions for its improvement. Dr. Eduard Radaceanu and Mrs. Doina Vladuca have done the same. The comments of Author, Professor, and National Public Radio commentator Andrei

Codrescu have been encouraging. My thanks also go to my wife, Barbara who was at my side during most of the Romanian experiences, to Lora Arnold and Alan Whitten for their valuable support and Dean C. David Billings, Dr. J. Daniel Sherman, and other members of the faculty and staff of the University of Alabama in Huntsville for providing the environment which allowed me to write this manuscript. I also want to express appreciation to the Romanian subjects, particularly Dana Munteanu (fictitious name) for their inputs. Without the information they provided, there would be no manuscript.
James K. McCollum
University of Alabama in Huntsville

Is Communism Dead Forever?

Chapter 1
Introduction

"Belarus backslides into old Soviet State," proclaims Georgie Anne Geyer in her column of January 5, 1998. She says that President Alexander Lukashenko of Belarus, "has a nasty, violent streak and a hatred for the West and for capitalism." He would like to come to power in Moscow as well as in Belarus and is trying to create conditions by which he and his supporters in Russia can prevail upon the demise of the Yeltsin government. Ms. Geyer states that similar regimes have emerged in Slovakia, Turkmenistan, and Uzbekistan.

The democracies of the world won the "Cold War" in 1989! But was it a complete victory? Is communism dead or is it merely in hiding until conditions become bad enough that it can reemerge? We know that communism is far from dead, because it still is the basis for the government of China, the world's largest country with 1.2 billion people. It also governs North Korea, Cuba, Vietnam, and Belarus. These are the overt bastions of communism, but there are others. The nations that made up the Soviet Union were under communism for more than seventy years; the nations of Eastern Europe were under communism for more than forty-four years. Many officials now governing in these nations held high government or communist party positions that gave them more status than they now command. Many older citizens who had spent their lives under the communist system feel that their reward for being good communists has been snatched away by this upstart democratic, free market movement that has turned their established world upside down.

What can these unhappy citizens do about their dislike of the new order? A lot! Their minions who still hold high offices in the new governments are able to stall progress toward privatization of state owned enterprises, restrict restructuring which allows them to become more profitable, and seriously harass entrepreneurs who are trying to take advantage of opportunities that exist. Slobodan Milosevic perpetrated a war in Yugoslavia to maintain his power in that country. Even after the break up of Yugoslavia, he has a lot of political power in the smaller Yugoslav federation.

Also problematical, nostalgic communists can continue the spy networks that existed under the communist governments and act as a "power behind the government" to continue to force favorable treatment for their own clique. For example, Lukashenko of Belarus has banned activities of private lawyers and has created legislation that allows his "special forces" the right to enter private homes without cause and to punish people for using their telephones in conversations that are against the interests of the state. These restrictions could be imposed in other former communist countries where leaders, even democratically elected leaders, feel threatened because they cannot control events and still have the proclivity to stifle opposition.

Life in the Newly Independent States

Imagine that you are an average citizen of Eastern Europe or the former Soviet Union. Until late 1989, as you lived your life under a communist government, your life was almost completely regulated by the "all knowing" communist party.[1] While the communist leaders told you that you lived in a worker's paradise, you had to stand in line for food items such as meat, milk, eggs, and bread and in lines for consumer goods such as soap, detergents and toilet paper. If you had a car, you waited in long lines for gasoline. Though your medical treatment was at no "official" cost, its value was not worthwhile unless you brought valuable presents to the doctors and nurses. Your education, too, was free, but it was outmoded and tightly controlled by the communist party.

The information you received through your local media was always contradicted by what you heard from clandestinely listening to the Voice of America and Radio Free Europe. You longed for a better environment, but could not travel outside the country and were not supposed to interact with foreigners who visited your country.

You had heard that any opposition to the communist government would bring swift, terrible punishment. You learned to survive, but you did not learn how to succeed in life.

Now, nine years after the end of formal communist control, most of the former conditions have changed. There is ample food in the stores, consumer goods on the shelves, gasoline in gas stations. You are able to interact with foreigners, openly receive news from all over the world, and to travel anywhere in the world. Life is now wonderful? No, not quite.

Almost everyone lives in small block apartments. Utility services are still turned off from time to time. You work in an outmoded, state owned factory, producing heavy equipment which often stays in finished products inventory for a long time. Your wages amount to about the equivalent of $80.00 per month and the prices in the markets are nearly the same as those paid by westerners. While it is true that your electricity, water, rent, and telephone charges are much less than those in the west, you still have trouble paying the bills.

Some citizens of your nation say their lives were better under communism. The government of Belarus has already reverted to a communist style dictatorship. The Poles, Hungarians, and Bulgarians have elected former communists to run their governments after having non-communists in charge. Why would anyone who survived the communist environment wish to return to the "bad old days" of communist repression and control? Will communism have a rebirth in the former Soviet empire, or could it emerge in "free world" countries?

The main purpose of this book is to show that the idea of a functional, successful communist society has proven to be a dead cocoon. However, there are still enough unrealistic dreamers who would like to try a communist system that makes this discussion relevant. I want to show here that a society based on a communist ideology cannot survive. It is because so many humans desire a guaranteed level of means of life that the lures of communism pose a continuing threat.

A sociologist once asked about one thousand different subjects to describe their ideas about perfect happiness. The sociologist and his subjects were living in a highly developed democratic country. A large portion of the subjects responded as follows:

- I want to have a house with at least three rooms and a car
- I want to be given a job that fits my education as soon as I graduate from school
- I want a free educational system
- I want free health care
- I want a good pension that covers all of my needs when I retire
- I want to have equal assets and privileges with my superiors so that I can never be humiliated no matter what place I am in the society.

The sociologist was shocked to discover in these responses a perfect description of the communist promises. This test tends to show that many people, by nature, are not competitive, but would like to receive everything in exchange for very little effort. For many who lived under it, this was what communism promised.

Those who lived under totalitarianism in the recent past, or still live under dictatorships today, need to be awakened and to be taught that life under democratic, free market conditions is superior to that under any dictatorship. We people from democratic countries do not claim to know everything about everything, but we want to help societies in transition because we feel responsible for those who are less fortunate. Communism can bring about horrific sagas in which millions of innocent people are killed simply because they are a nuisance for the ruling clique. A recently published *Black Book of Communism*[2] reported between 85 and 100 million deaths brought about by communist leaders who had no concern for the worth of human beings. If this figure doesn't cause readers any concern, it is understandable. Stalin once remarked, "A Single death is a tragedy. A million deaths is a statistic." And so, these thugs like Stalin, Pol Pot, Ceausescu, and Slobodan Milosevic have been getting away with murder under the name of communism for many years and only now do we have the chance to show how bad the face of communism was. Hopefully, people in democracies are still oriented toward eradicating this blight upon humanity.

President Clinton declared in his second inaugural address, "More people on this planet (now) live under democracy than dictatorship." According to statistics produced by the *New York Times*, 3.1 billion people live in democracies while 2.66 billion do not. While this is good news that people in democracies outnumber those in dictatorships, we must empathize with the 2.66 billion people in oppression. We should also remember the millions who are in transition from totalitarianism and lend them support.

* * *

My wife, Barbara, and I began a journey of discovery into Romania in September, 1991. At that time, I was very curious to know what we would find in a country beset by communism for almost forty-five years. Not quite two years had passed since the Romanian "Revolution" liberated the Romanian people from one of the most virulent communist dictators, Nicolae Ceausescu.

Once Ceausescu had been likened to Tito of Yugoslavia and called the "communist who is different" because of his opposition to the Soviet Union and refusal to send Romanian troops into Czechoslovakia in 1968. Hoping that he was leading the country toward a democratic, open society, President Nixon and Queen Elizabeth II rewarded him with state visits and high accolades. Unfortunately, after 1978, the news coming from Romania became increasingly dire. The regime from Bucharest was more correctly characterized by terms such as "hyper centralization," "state sponsored repression," and "police state."

Moving again to September, 1991, almost two years after the fall of the Ceausescu regime, I went to Romania as a Fulbright Scholar to teach business management to university students and practicing managers. My fellow Fulbrighters and I (there were twenty-one of us that year, the largest number ever sent to Romania) found a student and professional population that was eager to learn about democracy and free market conditions. Over a period of eleven months, I taught three university classes with 87 students in them and forty-five seminar-type classes to more than 1,000 practicing managers. Additionally, I conducted interviews and provided consulting assistance to hundreds of other business managers and government officials. I thought I had made at least a small impact on the Romanian world and its scant knowledge of free market management, but I knew that much more needed to be done.

The Romanians often told me that what they needed was a "Marshall Plan" of recovery assistance. I knew that the efforts being made by all of the agencies that were helping in the transition-

Fulbright Program, World Bank, International Monetary Fund, U.S. Information Agency, U.S. Agency for International Development, the British "Know-How" Fund, the European Union's Tempus Program, the PHARE Fund, and several private funds such as the Soros Foundation For an Open Society -- were not providing the same level of economic assistance given to western European countries under the Marshall Plan. However, the situation was different. Romania and the other Eastern European countries were not recovering from a shooting war with its toll of mass destruction, but rather from an ideological war that had changed the people's way of thinking and ways of doing things. Restructuring the economies in these former communist countries would mean more than simply reorganizing and privatizing the state owned businesses; it meant showing managers how to market their products or services, changing the mentality of the work force, and even proving to the older members of the population that doing business to make a profit is not immoral.

Over the next five years, I returned to Romania fifteen times to teach short courses, to work as a visiting professor, and to identify young middle-managers to bring to the U.S. for a management intern program. I taught seminars at the Black Sea University in Mangalia and at the Academy of Economic Studies and the Romanian Management Institute in Bucharest. For eight months, I was a visiting professor at the Lucian Blaga University in the beautiful medieval city of Sibiu. Within a program co-sponsored by the U.S. Information Agency, Soros Foundation for an Open Society, the University of Alabama in Huntsville, two Rotary Clubs, and several local businesses, I brought 53 Romanian middle managers to Huntsville, Alabama to work in some of our local enterprises.

Through all of this time, I observed Romanians closely and found that while some Romanians readily accept free market concepts, some do not. The presidency of Ion Iliescu, a former Ceausescu deputy, which lasted from December, 1989 to November, 1996, did not inspire rapid movement toward the free market. Old communist *nomenclatura* (the communist clique of high ranking party members and bureaucrats) still infested the government and both slowed privatization efforts and impeded entrepreneurs in the private sector.

The old industrial dinosaurs which should have been closed were kept alive and managers in state run enterprises were not held to the same standards of performance as were the managers in private enterprises.

Our U.S. trained interns who had been asked to share their knowledge with other managers reported a "mixed bag" in their attempts to enlighten others about free market management. This was revealed in a questionnaire they completed at a May, 1997 reunion in Bucharest of 42 of former interns. Almost all of them reported that while their individual careers were going well, they hadn't had much influence on their peers. Many associates and co-workers were envious of their intern experience, calling it a political plum that the interns were "lucky," or "well-connected," enough to get. In my perspective, the interns had earned the right to the internship through hard work and initiative so I thought the criticism was invalid. Later, with small groups of the former interns, I started having doubts. Some had suspected that a few of their fellow interns were working for the security apparatus of the Romanian government. After analyzing the behavior and speech of particular individuals, I began to accept the possibility that my dinner partners may have been right, some of the interns probably were informers. Several Romanian academicians contend that for every ten Romanians, another was, and probably still is an informer for the "political police" that rules the country from the shadows. This is a direct legacy of the old communist system.

Why should people spy on each other? We know it was happening in Ceausescu's Romania and in many other communist countries, but why now? Such activities are a great waste of time and the complete antithesis of democracy. But the old habits of communism are hard to kill. Iliescu, the former communist, wasn't interested in destroying them, even though these habits lead to corruption because they keep the leaders of the dying ideology functioning. It is only due to outside pressures that Iliescu allowed freedom of speech, freedom of the press, private TV stations, and passports for all citizens. These small portions of freedom were not going to endanger the *nomenclatura*.

Since November, 1996, the Romanian government has been led by a new president and prime minister from the Democratic Convention party which has a majority in a coalition government. After seven years of "freedom," it is the first democratic government since the communists took over in the 1940's and is having many difficulties in reshaping the country.

In July, 1997, Romania's desires to enter NATO and the

European Union were thwarted by President Clinton, although he did visit Bucharest on July 11, and gave the Romanians a psychological boost. According to the newspaper, *Ziua*, General Ion Mihai Pacepa, former assistant head of Romanian security under Ceausescu until his defection to the U.S. in 1978, wrote a letter in April, 1997, to Adrian Severin, the Romanian foreign minister, telling him that he had to dissolve the "political police" (informer network still in existence) and also to cancel the connections with the former KGB network if he expected Romania to get into NATO. *Ziua* reported that the foreign minister had ignored the warning, and this was probably the most important factor prohibiting NATO membership for Romania in the first wave of additional members.

Is communism being replaced gradually by a democratic system in Romania and other former communist countries, or are some of its tentacles still writhing around and stifling normal actions? Communism has been such a terrible scourge that we must not relax and assume that it will never reappear. Its effects on human beings are so pervasive and dreadful that we need to revisit its evils and how it evolves to make certain we keep the mordant monster discredited and weak. It needs to be described clearly in detail to make everyone aware of its faults in contrast with the benefits of political pluralism and openness in the democratic system. As poet Andrei Codrescu, who left Romania in the early 1970s, tells us in his 1986 book, *Comrade Past & Mister Present*,

> The great discovery of my thirties is plurality...
> In other words,
> all other words,
> not just the tolerance of difference,
> but the joyful welcoming of differences into one's heart spread
> out like the pages
> of a newspaper...

Currently, such pluralism does not exist in Romania and other newly independent states. There is still suppression of dissidence, all voices are not yet heard. Until such a condition exists, we must fear for the continuance of the nascent democracies.

Notes

1.   The Eastern European Soviet satellites began discarding their communist governments in November and December, 1989.   After the failure of the *coup d'etat* against Soviet President Mihail Gorbachev in August, 1991, the power of the Soviet communist party was broken and the former Soviet Union was converted into a "Commonwealth of Independent States" (CIS).

2.   Stephane Courtois, *Le Livre Noir du Communisme: Crimes Terreur Repression*. Paris: Centre Nationale de Research Scientifique, 1998.

Chapter 2

How Communism Came to One Eastern European Country

A near "worst case" example of the effects of communism can be seen in Romania. Romania is a nation of almost twenty-three million people[1], now second in size to Poland in Eastern Europe. Despite its significant size, it is virtually unknown to most Americans. When Americans are asked about Romania, they may say they know about "Aids babies" and Olympic champion Nadia Comaneci, but little else. There is, of course, much more to know about Romania, about its history, its culture, its scenic wonders, its business climate, its political environment. A big part of the reason for knowing about Romanians is to learn how they dealt with almost forty-five years of communism and how the nation is transitioning from a centrally-planned economy and communist government to a free market economy and democracy.

In a single word, we can characterize how the transition is going: "poorly." The years of communism have affected the mentality of a large portion of the population and the exportation of wealth from the country to pay for Ceausescu's massive "ego" projects have impoverished its natural riches and resources. Its greatest remaining asset is its people, but they have been suppressed and cowed into submission for so long that most of them are suspicious of programs to help them. The Ceausescu regime, along with those of Kim Il-Sung of North Korea and Enver Hoxha of Albania, were considered to be the most repressive of the communist regimes.

High Points of Romanian History

To better understand the Romanian situation, we should take a short look at Romanian history. Romania is made up of three large areas (sometimes designated as "principalities"): Wallachia (also called Tara Romaneasca and Muntenia at times in history)- the southern plains, Moldavia (Moldova)- the northeast, and Transylvania (Transilvanei)- the northwest, all of which are in Southeastern Europe between the 44th and 48th parallels of latitude and between the 21st and 29th meridians of East longitude.[2] These three sections were settled between 1800 and 800 B.C. by Thracian tribes called "Dacians" by the Romans who encountered them in the first century B.C. The lands of the Dacians, much of which were very fertile and produced prodigious crops, were conquered by the Roman empire under Emperor Trajan in 106 A.D., when Decebalus, the last Dacian king was defeated. The territory which is now Romania was under Roman control for more than 200 years.[3] During that time, many Romans and Dacians intermarried and Christianity became the established religion of the Romans and it also became the accepted religion of the "Romanian" people. Thus the language of the area was based on Latin, used in the marketplaces, in the churches, and eventually in all of the homes.

After the retreat of the Roman army and administration to the South side of the Danube river after 248 A.D., the area was invaded by a series of marauders: the Visigoths in 275 A.D., the Huns after 376 A.D., the Gepids in 454 A.D., the Avars in 567 A.D., and the Slavs in 602 A.D. Each of these groups ruled the inhabitants for a time, but was pushed out by another invading force. The Romanians stayed in their lands generally bounded by the Danube on the west and south, the Tisa River above the Carpathian mountains to the north, and the Black Sea and Prut River on the east. Their Latin-based language and Christian religion stayed with them, little changed by the departed invaders.[4] Romania eventually developed its own church hierarchy, called the Romanian Orthodox Church with its own Bishop.

Starting in the 9th century A.D., the Magyars (Hungarian descendants of the Huns) invaded from the north and many of them settled in the area now known as Transylvania, although they have never outnumbered Romanians in the principality. Subsequently, many German settlers called the "Szecklers" came later into Transylvania, establishing walled cities and churches. From the fifteenth century until well into the nineteenth century, Romania was dominated by the Ottoman Turks. In most instances, the domination amounted to paying large amounts of money to the Turks, although on a few occasions, Romanians won independence on the battlefield for some parts of the country and for brief periods, there was a unification of the three principalities. In the latter part of the 15th century, Stephen cel Mare of Moldavia was able to defeat the Turkish and the Polish invasions that were attempting to conquer all of the Romanian lands and tried to unite Moldavia with Transylvania. More than one hundred years later, Michael the Brave of Wallachia won several battles against the Ottoman Turks and was able to unify the three Romanian principalities: Wallachia (also called Muntenia), Transylvania, and Moldavia in 1600. The unification did not last long, but it impressed Romanians with the idea that all three countries should be together.[5] The first step to the permanent unification was made by Alexandru Ioan Cuza in 1859, when he united Moldavia and Muntenia into modern Romania.

In the 19th century, Transylvania was part of the Austro-Hungarian empire and the rest of Romania was a vassal of Turkey. Because Romanian statesmen were not satisfied with Ioan Cuza's policy, they decided that their destiny would be improved if they were ruled by a foreign king. To achieve this goal, a German prince, Karl of Hohenzollern-Sigmaringen was invited to become the king of unified Romania. Karl accepted and after the War of Independence, in 1877, against the Turks was won, he became King Carol the first of Romania.[6]

During World War I, Romania fought on the side of the Triple Entente powers, suffering many defeats and German occupation of much of its territory, but ultimately winning much in the aftermath of the war. Romania was given control of Transylvania, the Banat in the west, and some lands south of the Danube near the Black Sea called Dobrogea.[7]

Between the two world wars, the Romanian economy was very strong, and its currency was the most stable in all of Europe. Its agricultural output was exceptional. The land produced fabulous crops when in private hands, and made the country "the breadbasket of Europe" between the two world wars. The historian, Vlad Georgescu, tells us that, "between 1920 and 1940 Romania was fourth in Europe in area under cultivation, and was the fifth largest agricultural producer in the world."[8] Its government was then in the hands of the quixotic Carol II, son of King Ferdinand and Queen Marie and the nephew of King Carol I.

In the late 1930's, Romania established agreements with Britain and France to insure the country's territorial integrity. These agreements did not prevent Romania from losing Bessarabia (Romanian territories on the east bank of the Prut River) and Northern Bukovina (bordering the Ukraine) to the Soviet Union in 1940 due to the Molotov-Ribbentrop Pact of 1939 which also allowed Germany and the Soviet Union to divide Poland. Romania also lost Northern Transylvania to Hungary in 1940, by decree from Nazi Germany. Due to these unpopular events, King Carol II abdicated the throne to his son, Michael I, with Army Marshall Ion Antonescu brought in as Prime Minister to stabilize the country. Then at German request, Romania gladly invaded the Soviet Union with the Germans in June, 1941. The aim was to reclaim Bessarabia and Northern Bukovina.

Once the Romanian army was committed, it went forward with the Germans well beyond the territories it wanted to reclaim.[9] Romanian armies were on the Volga River at Stalingrad and deep in the Crimea at the time U.S. aid strengthened the USSR to the point where it could turn the tide of the war against the Axis.[10] The Romanian army was then steadily pushed back toward Romania by Soviet Forces and after Soviet armies were on Romanian territory,[11] Romania changed sides in the war. The Iron Guard leaders (Fascist sympathisers) were arrested on orders from King Mihai and the Romanian army began to fight against the Germans. "In a coup in August 1944, Michael had Antonescu arrested and declared Roumania [sic] on the side of the Allies. In doing this, the young King hoped to prevent the Soviet occupation of Roumania and help the Allies."[12]

Communism Comes to Romania

Even though Romania had changed sides, the aftermath of World War II found Romania with a Soviet army of occupation and many Soviet "advisers" helping develop what had been a very small (less than 1,000 member) Romanian Communist Party organization which took control of the government.[13]   Soviet manipulations brought communist leaders to power.   "Russia disarmed more than 100,000 Roumanian soldiers and confiscated much of the Roumanian fleet and merchant marine; railway stock, automobiles, and oil field supplies. Within less than a year, Andrei Vishinsky arrived in Bucharest, where he staged a Communist coup (February-March, 1945)."[14] Communist leaders won rigged elections in Romania in 1946, then on December 30, 1947, King Mihai was forced to abdicate his throne. Western leaders criticized the communists for forcing these changes against the will of the Romanian people, but took no overt actions. British Prime Minister Churchill was believed to have traded Romania to Stalin in return for the Soviet pledge to stay out of Greece. The test of that pledge was not long in coming as communist activists in Greece supported from the Soviet Union created such a threat to that country that without the "Truman Doctrine," enunciated in 1947, both Greece and Turkey would have soon been lost to communism.

Romania was lost to communism, not by the desire of the people, but by force of arms.   Once the communists were in power in Romania, they began converting the country to a Stalinist type of dictatorship.[15] Rather than "dictatorship of the proletariat," there was dictatorship over all classes of people by a small, but growing group of communists heavily supported by the Soviet Union. The intellectuals were particularly singled out for persecution by incarceration in the prisons of Sighetul-Marmetei or to work on the Danube River-Black Sea Canal. Many of them died in the two places of punishment.[16] Their offense against the communist government was that of having held monarchist or democratic ideals.

Property owners were also persecuted. In some areas, families were evicted from their houses and set out on bare land to try to survive.[17] Many of them did not survive the severe Romanian winter. In 1948, the so called "Marea Nationalizare" (Great Expropriation) took place: the communists closed all of the private banks, took control of all of the existing factories, workshops, services (restaurants, shops, warehouses, etc.) and more than eight hundred thousand private houses of all sizes.[18] The institution of private property was completely abandoned.

At the same time, systematic repression of churches was carried out. The Romanian Orthodox church was completely subordinated to the state and never acted to oppose the communists. A branch of Catholicism, called the Uniate Church, was forced to sever all ties with

Rome and unite with the Romania Orthodox Church. "The Uniate Church was Orthodox in its rites but accepted the spiritual authority of Rome."[19] Many members of the Orthodox, Uniate, and Jewish clergy were imprisoned or forced into exile.[20]

The farmers were also affected. Newly elected communist President Gheorghe Gheorhiu-Dej started collectivization of the family farms of Romania in 1947. The results were very poor and Georgescu tells us that by 1974, Romania "became a country with chronic food shortages."[21]

How could such a condition have come about in 27 years? It wasn't a problem with the weather as the North Koreans were claiming in 1997. The problem in Romania leading up to this state in 1974 was the collectivization of agriculture which destroyed incentives for the farmers. In the collective farms, the farmers were only allowed to sell animals to the state and would be fined or imprisoned if they slaughtered animals for private use. The farmers were allowed to keep only a small amount of the grain from the collective farms. Besides, labor on the collective farms was so poorly managed that there usually were not enough workers to harvest the produce and much of it rotted in the fields.

Forced industrialization took many of the young people out of rural areas and into the cities. Gheorghe-Gheorghiu-Dej and Ceausescu after him, were determined that Romania would not simply have an agricultural economy, as was encouraged by the Soviet Union. Dej and Ceausescu wanted Romania to be self sufficient in manufacturing and to this end, they brought in outside technologies, both from communist and noncommunist countries, to allow Romania to have heavy industries and become an "industrial" nation. Engineering and physical sciences were promoted in the universities, as well as the liberal arts. More engineers were needed for the factories and more teachers were needed for a larger population of children. Romania's communist leaders tried to emulate the Stalinist model of economy and government in most respects. By the 1980's, Romania had one of the largest steel producing capacities in the world with huge integrated steel mills at Galati, Resita, Hunedoara, Calan, Calarasi, and Tirgoviste.[22] It had one of the largest capacities for machine tools in the world. Automobiles of three types, locomotives, rail cars, armored cars and many supporting products were manufactured in Romania, although few of the factories were producing efficiently. However, consumer goods were given a very low priority.

In a very insightful and frightening book, *Red Horizons: Chronicles of a Communist Spy Chief*, published in 1987, Ion Mihai Pacepa reported that Ceausescu's philosophy was, "We should not direct our industrial potential toward producing toilet paper and kitchen appliances. . . Let that be a task for future generations. Space radars and high-powered laser weapons are what we should put our efforts into. Today, we have enough intelligence strength to obtain those American secrets. That would make us the most important and respected Soviet partner in the Warsaw pact tomorrow."[23] This very clearly shows the communist leaders were not aware of their limitations and they had unrealistic expectations about their technological power. They never took into account the need for proper stimulation for creativity and even expressed disdain for talented inventors, scientists and researchers.

A huge bureaucracy grew up with the centralized planning that was occurring to bring the collectivization of the farms, industrialization with all of its demands for people to be transplanted from rural areas to the cities, strict control of transportation, recreation, tourism and all other facets of life. Georgescu[24] states, "All decisions, even minor ones, were typically being referred to the highest levels." This hyper-centralization caused bottlenecks and many incorrect decisions to be made, particularly during the Ceausescu presidency.

Nicolae Ceausescu had emerged as the new President of Romania a few days after the death of Gheorghe Gheorghiu-Dej in 1965 and at first he was viewed by the outside world as an improvement over his predecessor. Pavel Campeanu, who had been a fellow prisoner with Ceausescu first in the Jilava military prison in 1941 and later in the Carasebes Special Penitentiary in 1942, said of Ceausescu that his most striking feature was his deep hatred for his fellow inmates.[25] Soon, the Romanian people would learn that he also had no regard for them and he treated them as his pawns or slaves.

In the Spring of 1968, Ceausescu refused to send Romanian troops to suppress Alexander Dubzec's attempt to open Czechoslovakia to outside ideas. This act gave Ceausescu much acceptance in the west. Perhaps, the most striking result was that Romania was visited by President Richard Nixon in 1969. Not long after, Ceausescu was knighted by the Queen of England and was invited to the White House in Washington. Had he died in 1971, he would probably be revered by the Romanian people. Instead, he increased his efforts to control the lives of Romanians, down to prescribing what their diets should be.

Of much greater import, Pacepa, who was called to confer with Ceausescu on a daily basis, stated that Ceausescu was handing out death sentences through his *Securitate* apparatus which operated on a worldwide basis as well as in Romania. Ceausescu, whose formal education ended in grammar school, but continued in his self study of Marxism-Leninism-Communism, could not accept any criticism of his handling of Romanian affairs and he was especially incensed toward Radio Free Europe and its commentators. He wanted his spies to find ways to blow up the station and kill the personnel. At one point his censors had intercepted some anonymous letters addressed to Radio Free Europe criticizing the Ceausescus' "personality cult." In a fit of rage, Ceausescu ordered his security chiefs to get samples of the handwriting of every school child and adult Romanian so that their handwriting experts could identify who had written the letters. Additionally, he wanted every typewriter owned by the state registered with the *Securitate* along with a sample of its type. A new decree forbade the renting or lending of typewriters and the ownership of a typewriter required special authorization.[26]   One official questioned whether making private citizens register their typewriters might be unconstitutional. Ceausescu handled that eventuality by saying, "Did the Constitution make us, or did we make it? We made the Constitution. We'll change it if we have to."[27]

Ceausescu was worried because the economy became very poor and he paid off the external debts with food products, the only merchandise that was accepted by foreign markets. For this reason, he was force to introduce the food rationing program. Since the meat, the cereals, the cheese, and the butter were going to Russia and fruit and vegetables to Germany and the former Yugoslavia, there was no more food for the population. People in the cities could survive only by getting help from relatives in the countryside. Farmers in the countryside were very restricted in what they could keep, but they worked very hard so they could save some food for their city relatives.

Once the rationing began, each Romanian family was issued a ration card. The families were designated to go to only one grocery store where they could buy food and could present their ration card at that store. Meanwhile, Ceausescu's agricultural ministry was forcing the farmers to give the state almost all grain produced and animals born and would prosecute any farmer who held out more grains or meats for themselves than allowed. The announced reason for rationing was that there was a food shortage, but at the same time, Romania was exporting meats and grains outside the country to earn hard currency for Ceausescu's building projects. Campeanu states, "Food and medical treatment were not withheld out of necessity but because of Ceausescu's cruel and deliberate schemes to pay off the country's foreign debts and to control the population. Central to these schemes were the scorn and hatred that were part of Ceausescu's character."[28]

Another means of obtaining hard currency was through selling citizens who wanted to emigrate. Andrei Codrescu informs us that the West German and Israeli governments were paying up to $10,000 per person to allow them to leave Romania. Codrescu himself had been ransomed by the Israeli government and eventually made his way to America[29] Romania's loss was our fortunate gain. Pacepa indicated that there was a sliding scale and valuable individuals might cost Israel as much as $50,000 to get someone out of Romania.[30]

At the same time, very little was being spent to provide decent lives for the Romanian people. In addition to rationing their food, health care was very poor. While the care available was at no cost to the citizens, it was not worth very much. Pacepa was describing the life of the *nomenclatura* and entered onto the subject of health care: "The darker the car, the closer the house is to Ceausescu's vacation residence, and black car people also get cooks and servants. They do not stand in line outside Soviet-style polyclinics, where treatment is free but you are yelled at by everyone from the doorman on up and may not spend more than 15 minutes with the doctor, who has to see at least 30 patients in his eight-hour shift. They do not go to the regular hospitals, where people may have to double up two to a bed. They have the luxurious, Western-style hospitals, built as a private foundation in the days before Communism."[31]

If we overlook the degrading policy of making women allow themselves to be examined for pregnancy each month, probably the worst Ceausescu program was that of thought control. Ceausescu came to believe that it was "scientific government" to be able to know what the people were saying when they believed they were having private conversations. He could not conceive the concept of "repression" of people's personalities caused by the fear induced by knowledge that anything anyone said could and would be recorded and used against them to show that they were "enemies of the people." Ceausescu's Chief of Security in the 1970's, General Pacepa was given the orders to have people both inside Romania and abroad beaten up or have fatal accidents because of their dissident views. Eventually, Pacepa could not stomach the odious job he was being forced to do and he defected to the U.S. in July 1978. Pacepa had lists of the Romanian spies all over the world which he provided to the CIA after his defection. Ceausescu's spy network was destroyed and with the information of the dictator's methods and paranoia, Ceausescu was never again invited to a Western country or given any status as a statesman by westerners.

In his book, *Red Horizons: Chronicles of a Communist Spy Chief*, Pacepa described a visit Nicolae Ceausescu and wife, Elena, made to an exhibit of technical surveillance devices at the Communist Party's Central Headquarters in Bucharest. According to Pacepa, "In 1965, when Ceausescu became the supreme leader, population monitoring grew into a mass operation of unprecedented scope. Hundreds of thousands of new microphones were silently put to work from their hiding places in offices and bedrooms, starting with those of the Politburo. As in the Soviet Union or in any other Communist country, corruption and prostitution reigned at the highest levels in Romania, and the microphones relentlessly recorded everything." The Ceausescu's were very interested in the many "bugging" devices they were shown at the exhibit. They asked how many people could be monitored at the end of the next five-year plan (1984) and were told that ten million could be monitored simultaneously if the organization's proposals were approved.

Ceausescu ended the meeting with a pep talk for the bugging organization, "For the past decade, each year has marked something new in our Communist history. Let us make 1984 another cornerstone. Let us again be unique in the Warsaw Pact. Let us be the first in the entire world, comrades. In a very short time we will be the only country on earth able to know what every single one of its citizens is thinking. . . Why is American imperialism so unpopular? Because it does not know what its people think. . . The Communist system we are creating together is the most scientific ever, I repeat comrades, *ever* to be put at the service of mankind."

General Pacepa capped this discussion by saying, "Every East European country has its own top secret 'Iosif's unit,' (the organization close to Ceausescu which monitored the microphones day and night and gave Ceausescu reports on what all of the high-ranking government and party officials said in the previous 24 hours) where a faceless army of little security people record everything for the supreme leader, even the way a *nomenclatura* man moans when he is making love."[32] Ceausescu apparently believed that he was doing a better job of monitoring his citizens than any of the other communist dictators. Unfortunately, a generation of "faceless" men who performed that kind of work are still around to use their knowledge of the frailties of others against them.

As a result of the paranoia against anyone having ideas that conflicted with those of the communist regime, individuals who had conversations with foreigners had to go to the police stations to make reports of these conversations. Where dissidence was found, it was ruthlessly punished. Many individuals were put on trial and sentenced either to death or to prison for speaking against the regime. When a massive strike by the miners occurred in the Jiu Valley in 1977, it was brutally stopped by the Army and Securitate and some of its leaders were summarily executed. The same fate occurred to leaders of an abortive strike in Brasov ten years later.[33]

At about the same time as the visit to the bugging organization presented by General Pacepa, Ceausescu visited North Korea and saw the "cult of personality" developed by Kim Il Sung. Ceausescu decided that he wanted such adoration for himself and directed his sycophants to put it into play. After that, he became the "Most Beloved Son of The People," idolized at parades and rallies. His wife, Elena, who was actually the number two in power got similar amounts of "adoration."[34]

Conditions worsened during the 1980's, with less and less food and creature comforts available to the average Romanian, while the ruling class of high level communists and securitate operatives lived very well. Average Romanians stood in long lines for days and nights in the rain, wind, and snow to buy milk, meat, cheese, and other foodstuffs that were normally in abundance in the country before the beginning of the economic failure. We can say, as a sad joke, that the industrial dinosaurs and the megalomanical palaces were "eating" all of the resources. Motorists sat in long lines to obtain gasoline for their cars, more than that, cars were restricted from being driven on Sundays: one Sunday, cars with even numbered license plates could be driven, the next Sunday, only cars with odd numbers. In the winters, there was no heat in the apartments of average people and insufficient natural gas pressure for them to cook their food until after midnight,[35] besides, the electricity was stopped for at least two hours per day in Bucharest and for many more hours all over the country. In the villages, people would have only three hours of electricity for the entire day. No hot running water but for two hours per day. The answer to these problems, in addition to increased surveillance to punish people who complained, was to establish "Food Factories" where Romanians would go to eat their meals of the number of calories prescribed by their leader. The shells of four of these monstrosities sit unfinished in Bucharest today as testimony to the utter lack of consideration Ceausescu had for his people. Of course, Ceausescu and his ruling class of "yes men" and *securitate* thugs were not destined to eat in the Food Factories. Pacepa tells us that the inner clique of communist party elite and *securitate* members, the *nomenclatura*,[36] had special stores where they bought their food which was abundant for them. Some of them could even telephone for home delivery.

In December 1989, after the fall of the Berlin Wall and the fall of communism in most of Eastern Europe, a rebellion against Ceausescu occurred in Romania. Beginning in Timisoara, it soon spread to other cities. Ceausescu ordered his army and security elements to quash the rebellion with force, but instead of stopping it, the rebellion grew and is now called the Romanian Revolution. Initially, the *securitate* forces killed many protesters in Timisoara, including women and children, but the army would not fire on protesters.[37]   There were many gun battles in the cities against an unknown and unseen enemy and much destruction of property, but the official reason for the battles was that security agents were fighting to preserve the dictator and the army was opposing them.

While trying to flee from Bucharest on December 22, 1989, Ceausescu and his wife were arrested near Targoviste and tried before a military tribunal, then rapidly executed by the *Securitate*. That was because the Ceausescus knew too much information (foreign bank accounts, names, figures, key words) about those who were assuming governmental control under a democratic mask.[38] Ceausescu knew in detail about those capable of manipulating large amounts of money to get the financial power and to quickly develop a mafiotic type of network based on corruption and total disdain for the laws.

Notes

1. Comisia Nationala Pentru Statistica, *Anuarul Statistic Al Romaniei 1993* (Bucharest: Imprimeriilor Coresi, 1994), p. 91. The total population given in this publication is 22,810,035.

2. Mircea Dogaru and Mihail Zahariade, *History of the Romanians: From the Origins to the Modern Age*, (Bucharest: Amco Press Publishing House, 1996), p. 3. The area now occupied by Romania is about the same as that of the combined states of Georgia and Alabama.

3. Vlad Georgescu, *The Romanians: A History*, (Columbus: Ohio University Press, 1991), p. 6. (Authors's note) The historical treatment I am providing is very sketchy and only to give the reader who has no knowledge of Romania some feel for the Romanian early development. For a more complete understanding of the Romanians, I would refer you to a book like that referenced in this foot note.

4. Dogaru and Zhariade, pp. 108-118.

5. Hannah Pakula, *The Last Romantic: A Biography of Queen Marie of Roumania*, (New York: Simon and Schuster, Inc., 1985). p. 76, "The unification of this triple kingdom, which corresponds roughly to present day Roumania, lasted less than a year, but it served as inspiration for centuries of Roumanians." ("Roumania" is a turn of the century English spelling of the name)

6. Ibid., pp. 77-85.

7. Tom Gallagher, *Romania After Ceausescu: The Politics of Intolerance*, (Edinburgh: Edinburgh University Press, 1995), p. 22. "After 1918, the pre-war "Old Kingdom" or *Regat* more than doubled its size and population."

8. Georgescu, p. 198.

9. Gallagher, p. 47, states, "Antonescu committed himself wholeheartedly to the German cause. Romania stayed in the war after all of Bessarabia had been recaptured and, by 1943, with the war clearly going against the Axis, the Romanian casualty rate was approaching 500,000.

10. *West Point Atlas of American Wars*, Map 41, World War II, 1959. "During the war, the United States alone provided Russia with 385,883 trucks, 51,503 jeeps, 7,056 tanks, 5,071 tractors, 1,981 locomotives, 11,158 freight cars, and 14,874 airplanes. Other supplies included 2,670,00 tons of petroleum products, industrial plants and equipment, and enough food to give each Russian soldier over one-half pound of fairly concentrated food per day."

11. Ibid. "The Russians entered Bucharest on 1 September (1944)."

12. Pakula, *The Last Romantic*, p. 433.

13. George Schopflin, *Politics in Eastern Europe: 1945-1992*. Oxford: Blackwell Publishing Company, 1993, p. 66.

14. Pakula, *The Last Romantic*, p. 433.

15. George Schopflin, *Politics in Eastern Europe.* Schopflin's description of a "Stalinist" type of government included a rejection of feedback - no criticism of any government decisions was possible. There was also a dependence upon terrorism to keep the people under control.

16. Vlad Georgescu, *History of the Romanians.* p. 236.

17. Traian Golea, *Romania: Beyond the Limits of Endurance*, Miami Beach: Romanian Historical Studies, 1988. "In June, 1951, the government stepped in to cut off their (partisans against the communist regime) basis of support by massive deportations. In every village, all inhabitants suspected of disloyalty to the regime or sympathy with protesting groups were arrested and deported either in the open steppes of the Baragan or in Moldavia, in the open field, with no structure to protect them from the bitter winter and no material support;" pp. 29-30.

18. In 1997, Prime Minister Victor Ciorbea's cabinet was trying to settle 800,000 requests for lost property.

19. Gallagher, p. 12.

20. Georgescu, p. 237.

21. Ibid, p. 259.

22. Dan Ionescu, "Romania: The A to Z of the Most Polluted Areas," *Report on Eastern Europe* (May 10, 1991), pp. 20-25. The forced industrialization was performed with little or no concern for the environmental damage that resulted. Today, the Romanian government is very careful to prevent new industries from causing additional pollution, but the existing legacy will take many years to correct.

23. Ion Mihai Pacepa, *Red Horizons, Chronicles of a Communist Spy Chief,* p. 46.

24. Georgescu, p. 270.

25. Pavel Campeanu, "The Revolt of the Romanians," *The New York Review* (February 1, 1990), p. 1.

26. Andrei Codrescu, *The Hole in the Flag*, (New York: William Morrow and Company, Inc., 1990), p. 120.

27. Pacepa, pp. 199-200.

28. Campeanu, p. 2.

29. Andrei Codrescu, *The Life and Times of an Involuntary Genius*, (New York: A Venture Book, 1975), p. 126.

30. Pacepa, p. 75.

31. Ibid., pp. 171-72.

32. Ibid., p. 205.

33. Campeanu, p. 2.

34. In a transcript of the trial of the Ceausescus which took place on December 25, 1989, Ceausescu states that Elena is "First Deputy Prime Minister."

35. Campeanu, p. 1 and Gallagher, pp. 61-65.

36. Ion Mihai Pacepa, *Red Horizons*, p. 171. Pacepa relates, "To the ordinary Romanian people, the word *nomenclatura* means the elite, a social superstructure recognizable by its privileges. *Nomenclatura* people do not travel by bus or streetcar. They use government cars...*Nomenclatura* people do not live in apartment buildings constructed under the Communist regime. As I did, they get nationalized villas or luxury apartments that previously belonged to the capitalists. *Nomenclatura* people are not seen standing in line to buy food or other necessities. They have their own stores..."

37. Sorin Alexandru, "The Challenge of Power," *The Times Literary Supplement* (19-25 January, 1990), pp. 55-56. Alexandru wrote, "I walked into a dream world: tanks in the streets were not firing on people but hunting down Securitate on behalf of the people, graffiti on the Intercontinental Hotel stating, "Communism is dead. Throw away your membership card."

38. Edward Behr, *Kiss the Hand You Cannot Bite: The Rise and Fall of the Ceausescus*, (New York: Villard Books, 1991), pp. 17-27.

Chapter 3

Living Under the Communist System: Case Study

When they graduated from their universities in the middle of the 1950's, Dana Munteanu's[1] parents were assigned to work in Giurgiu, a small town on the Danube, where Dana was born. After two years, they were transferred to Bucharest. Although they had good jobs in Bucharest, they did not have a place of their own to live in with minimum decent conditions. They were sent to a very old block of flats that had been built in 1914 and had been expropriated by force from its legal owners a short time before the parents moved in. What had once been a very elegant apartment with a large, round living room, four bedrooms, and a small servant's room, a kitchen and a bathroom was then divided among three families who were perfect strangers to each other.

Once the apartment belonged to the state, it rapidly became a ruin, because none of the dwellers would take the responsibility to repair it and to keep it in good shape. The staircase was very deteriorated, according to Dana's first memories when she was four years old. The outside of the house desperately needed repainting. The space that had been a merry living room was then deserted and bare -with no pictures on the walls, no furniture and only a faded old carpet on the floor. These sad images, together with the first questions, "Mommy, why can't we go to the kitchen?"

"Because we have to wait for the others to finish their dinner."

Or, "Mother, I have to go to the bathroom."

"You can't go now.   Someone else is using it.   Use the chamberpot under the bed," are also among Dana's first memories.

The child felt extremely depressed and knew that something was terribly wrong.   She knew it was wrong because her grandparents had very nice houses of their own with large kitchens.   But she wouldn't say anything because the family had to whisper all of the time, so they wouldn't disturb the other apartment dwellers.   Besides that, the little girl was told, "Whenever you go and play outdoors, be sure you never mention anything we discuss in private in our house.."

She would ask, "Why is that?"

The answer came like a sword, "Because it is *dangerous.*"

"What was so dangerous?" the reader might inquire.   The political police, organized according to the KGB model, was already in existence and in full function.   The members of the *Securitate* were always glad to deliver to the "Great Inquisitor" any "witch" they might discover.   A new "witch hunt" had started under a new cruel period of Inquisition.   Whoever dared to speak of freedom, monarchy, friends from the free world and about many other forbidden subjects would be put into prison immediately as being a real threat "for the smooth development of communism."

So the first thing she knew about the world, was that there was a big danger in the street.   Instead of being afraid, she was extremely curious.   She started to talk to her grandparents:

"Tell me, grandma, why is it so dangerous to speak freely to your friend about everything you would like to say?"

"Because these days, dear child, there are a lot of mean, envious people, that would like to destroy your family since your parents have good jobs and somebody would like to take these jobs for themselves."

"But, we are not discussing anything important in the house."

"Everything is important.   If you mention that your grandpa is a priest, somebody would think that your parents go to church, or have icons in the house.   I'm old and can go to the church, but your parents cannot.   Your parents are the young generation, the communist generation.   But, if you want, I can tell you beautiful stories about my generation and my parent's generation and my grandparent's generation."   Our subject was surprised to learn that her grandmother in Sighet used to have two servants to help her with housekeeping and a beautiful black carriage driven by two strong horses.   Like in fairytales, grandma was going by carriage to numerous balls organized by the mayor of the city. All of this serene and beautiful life could be enjoyed back in the twenties and thirties. At that time, people had a stronger sense of morality and gentility. We can conclude that communism abruptly interrupted the normal course of development toward democracy. Romania could have been like France today without this catastrophe.

The young couple waited for three years in those awful conditions in the shared apartment in Bucharest before they could get a place of their own where they could have privacy and intimacy. Then in 1960, they received a very small apartment for themselves with one bedroom, one living room, a very small kitchen, and a very small bathroom. After 13 years, it became their own apartment. Until 1973, all of the apartments belonged to the state. Then in 1973, the communist leaders wanted a source of money and decided to sell the apartments to their occupants and the couple bought theirs.

Meanwhile, our subject went on finding out all of the marvelous stories about the four families, from which the grandparents were coming. She found out that she was one quarter Hungarian from her grandfather, the priest and one quarter Greek from her grandfather in Braila.

We had met Dana, the subject of this case study, while she was working as an executive secretary in a private training institution. We asked what her previous job had been. She said she had been a training officer at a state owned factory for 10 years, but she was so happy when the revolution took place that she decided to find a job in a private company as soon as possible. She was extremely oriented toward a democracy based on a free market economy and she wanted everything to change very quickly. She once told us, "Romania is too rich and too beautiful to be abandoned by God."

Although we have spoken to many Romanians about their lives under the communist system prior to writing this case study, we had only fragmentary accounts. Some individuals had talked about such anomalous activities as being taken out of their factories to use pails of water to irrigate parched farming areas. Others discussed the wasted hours spent standing in long lines to buy meat, milk, or even bread. It is difficult to bring life to these fragmentary pictures. We found Dana, who was willing to describe her life in more depth over a period of several months of questioning and recording, often causing pain to her as she remembered details she would like to have forgotten. But some of the memories, particularly of her family, were pleasant.

Family Background and Early Life

The subject considers that she was lucky to have been born into a good family. Her mother's parents were from Braila, an important port on the Danube. Up to the communist era, Braila was the biggest port in Europe for international trading in cereals, the price of wheat for all of Europe was established by Braila's market. It was also an important port for trading various goods from other countries, especially from Greece and Turkey and some Greeks and Turks had established their homes and businesses in Braila. Through these sailors and tradesmen, citizens of Braila had access to information from the rest of the globe which provided them with an open-minded approach to looking at the world.

Subject's Mother's Family

Maternal Grandfather: A genuine Greek, dealing in the fur trade and coats who left his family (parents and sister - Papadopolous) in Greece and developed his business in Braila. He established a small, but profitable fur workshop then married a Romanian lady whose father was also of the middle-class, the owner of a barrel workshop. The husband entered the marriage with the fur workshop; the wife with a small, nice house in the center of the city.

Maternal Grandmother: She came from a well-to-do family that had five children for whom the father was able to support well through his successful barrel workshop. Unfortunately, after ten years of a good marriage and two children and a good business development, the Greek husband developed a mental disease caused by the shock of losing his business during the Second World War and the couple divorced. After a short period of trying to earn a living by herself, the lady remarried a good-hearted gentleman who accepted her and the two children.

The important aspects here are: Subject's mother was half Greek and even if she couldn't stay in touch with relatives in Greece, the Greek religion and history were an important influence on the family. Dana believed that all persons described above, without being rich, were satisfied with their decent lifestyles and happy with the normal development toward democracy taking place after the First World War. They all belonged to the important middle-class that gives stability to a democratic society.

Second husband (the grandfather our Subject knew): The grandfather was a master mason in the home building trade and he was able to provide good support for his wife and two children. They owned a nice house with a courtyard near the center of the city. The wife spent her life taking care of the house and the children, giving them a good education She never worked at a job because in those times, women were not supposed to work if their husbands could provide for the family. When communism suddenly came upon them, they didn't lose their three room house because it was not large enough to be divided for another family. Since they didn't lose anything, they accepted the change of the regime with serenity and indifference and their lives did not change very much. The grandfather, being well skilled in home building, was able to obtain a good job in a state enterprise and was able to continue to support his family.

When the communist regime began, both children had graduated from high school and both had been accepted in universities because they were children of a worker. Both children developed good careers in the communist era: the daughter graduated from the Academy of Economic Studies in Bucharest and worked for thirty-two years as a high school teacher. The son graduated from the Military Academy in Bucharest and served until retirement with the rank of Colonel.

Subject's Father's Family

Paternal Grandparents: The subject's paternal grandparents were from Sighetul Marmatiei in Transilvania in the north of Maramures county at the border with the Ukraine and Hungary. Therefore, there were lots of Hungarians and a few Ukrainians living with the Romanians in the peaceful town which looks like a German burg, The grandfather was a Greek-Catholic (Uniate) priest. The grandmother was an emancipated woman who decided to have her own career, so she worked as an executive secretary to the City Hall. She also was the daughter of a Greek-Catholic priest and had a good education. The couple had two servants to help with their five children and a horse carriage for transportation.

When communism came, the grandfather was clever enough to forecast the future and sold his assets which included land in the countryside and the horses and carriage and immediately agreed to become an Orthodox priest. For most of the priests, it was extremely painful to change their religious affiliation overnight even though Orthodoxy is another strong branch of Christianity. Some of those who refused were executed. Others tried a combination of the two Christian rituals, but they never again were in contact with the Pope up until the revolution in 1989. Actually, the great majority of the population of Maramures didn't change their religious traditions because they were too far from Bucharest politics to understand and change beliefs that had prevailed for centuries. The communists had banned the Greek-Catholic rite because they didn't want to have any connection with the Pope in Rome, but they allowed the Romanian Orthodox Church to continue to function, on the condition that the priests would become informers for *Securitate* and they would perform very formal services in the church with no strong spiritual message.

The grandmother, as the former executive secretary of the mayor, turned out to be very useful for the new communist rulers. She knew everything about everything from the town records and later became a member of the communist party. However, the grandfather and grandmother made these changes in their lives in the interest of their children. They actually hated the communist system, but were willing to sacrifice their principles to save their children. So they did. All five children graduated from universities: the father of the subject became a prosecutor after graduating *magna cum laude* from the law school in Cluj. While he was still a student at the university in Cluj, he participated in a student summer camp for meritorious students where he met the subject's mother who was then in her last year at the Academy of Economic Studies in Bucharest. They liked each other and decided to get married.

* * *

One day in 1960, as a little girl of five, Dana came home from a visit to Braila with her grandmother to see her parent's new apartment. Her father was waiting for them at the *Gara du Nord* (Main Bucharest Train Station, built between 1914 and 1919). It was a summer evening that she would never forget: first of all, because her father hailed a taxi and for the first time in her life, she traveled by car and second, coming from quiet Braila she was shocked by noise and all of the lights. It seemed that the whole city was on fire. It was so beautiful that even the little apartment made her extremely happy, although there was no room in it for her privacy. These new apartments were meant for some of the important government employees. On the same floor lived a prosecutor, a judge, and two workers in important communist party administration positions. Those apartments were completely furnished with carpets, curtains, furniture, and a phone - everything provided free, because these were considered as service dwellings. They were like hotels.

The location of the apartment was amazing - it was very near the Congress Hall and the Royal Palace. The family used to take strolls in the evening around the Royal Palace and there was an ocean of lights showing that communism is glorious. More than that, she was very impressed by a sophisticated fountain that covered one wall of a block of apartments built by Americans in the 1920's. This building was located in front Central Committee of the PCR (Communist Party of Romania). What is extremely strange is that fifteen years later, no one could remember that the fountain had ever existed. It existed at least until 1965.[2] Why was this fountain so special? Because its jets of water were as tall as the building and put in operation in the evening together with very powerful colored search lights illuminated the water in the most pleasing nuances, light blue, light yellow, light violet, light green, pink, light orange, changing all of the time- fairy like and very enchanting.

After she'd had spent a lot of time with her grandmother in Braila, the little girl knew a lot of things about the former history of the country and about religion. She learned most of the details about the former kings of Romania and a lot of information about King Michael who had been forced to abdicate in spite of the fact that the majority of the people loved and appreciated him. She got familiar with the Bible and she was shocked to learn that every morning the students, during her grandmother's time, started their day in school with the Lord's Prayer and then sang the National Anthem. Her grandmother told her the whole truth about what was going on in the society under the new regime, but she encouraged her to never lose her faith in God so she would not become desperate under this system.

This encouragement made her thank God for providing her the best location in the center of Bucharest, near the Royal Palace, near the Cismigiu Gardens, near the Hotel Lido pool with its artificial waves. The Lido Garden Restaurant that surrounded the Lido Pool was like an island from the capitalist Western Europe. Even though she was only nine years old, whenever she had the opportunity to go there, she felt like Greta Garbo, Bette Davis or Catherine Hepburn., or some other actress that she had seen in movies such as The Maltese Falcon or Casablanca.

Once the family was in the new apartment and in the new location, she thought that maybe communism was not so bad after all. The nearby stores were filled with merchandise and the groceries had plenty of meat, all kinds of cheeses, and other foodstuffs.

However, she was a little confused when seeing her grandfather, the bricklayer, become irritated while listening to the radio news. The voice in the radio was saying, "Our successful tractors were able to complete a marvelous work in the field. The peasants were happy to report that they finished the ploughing and the sowing."

At this, the grandfather would begin to shout, "Liars, Liars, You communists are a bunch of liars!"

And the little girl was too little to ask questions, but the grandfather knew well from his brother in the countryside that the peasants had been forced to give up their lands and their tools and integrate their assets in the CAP (*Cooperativa Agricola de Productia*) collective farms and everybody felt depressed and dispossessed.

Early Education
While the best intellectuals of the country were exterminated and exiled to prisons and at the canal, having no direct source of information, Dana didn't personally notice any cruelties in her early years.   She was lucky again as she started to school.   It was announced that she was to be a student in an experimental class. The experiment was that of having different teachers for the different subjects beginning in the first grade, which normally, in Romania, has one teacher for all subjects who stays with that class for four years.   Therefore, she had no time to become bored and on the contrary she became aware that it is extremely interesting and useful to have different teachers for each subject because they represented different models for the future in life. There were both men and women, young teachers and old teachers, a variety of voices, a variety of clothes and this was very inspiring for the children.

Every day was new, every day was special from a certain point of view: Teacher for the Romanian history told the students wonderful legends about the Romanian people in the past and would bring pictures to show how art was inspired by the historical events. Music Teacher would bring records to the class and they all enjoyed listening to classical music. Nature and Geography Teacher would bring splendid albums with flowers and animals and wonderful postcards of Romanian scenery. They called this "active school" when teachers would include the students in the learning process, encouraging them: "If you happen to have at home post cards, pictures, good music records, or anything else of interest concerning our subjects of interest, bring them to school and let us share the information." It was a real pleasure for her to come to school, but as we said at the beginning, Dana was in an experimental class. The communist leaders decided to terminate it, she believes, because the experiment turned out to be too good and too encouraging for the children. They became aware that under such a good educational system, the students would start to think too much and too deeply. Her belief now is that, "The one who thinks a lot would never accept life under a communist system. Communism needs stupid robots, not intelligent thinkers."

When she was in grammar school, the students were highly motivated to learn. Everything seemed very well organized in the school. Everything was clean, even the toilets were clean. The children were told to bring their lunches. The teachers would send them to wash their hands, then during the lunch break, they would eat the sandwiches and fruit they brought from home. There was a general atmosphere of respect and discipline in the school. Everyone wore clean uniforms. The teachers even checked the children's handkerchiefs. The young students were motivated to study hard because they all wanted to become a member of the Young Pioneer Organization. Our subject developed a strong sense of justice because she noticed that the grades were reflecting the real value of each student. None was receiving special favors for no good reasons. In order to become a member of the Young Pioneer organization, a student had to place among the first five students of the class in the third grade, which created real competition among the students. Dana did not place well enough in the third grade, but was able to become a pioneer in the 4th grade.

So, Dana was happy with her little apartment, her school, her teachers, and all of the marvels that Bucharest provided her. Among these beauties was the Christmas Children's Town, which came like a special treat at the end of the year and, because all religious feasts were not allowed under communism, all of the names were changed. "Christmas Town" was replaced "Little Children's Town," "Father Christmas" by "Father Frost" and the "Christmas tree" became the "Winter tree." Workers usually began building the Christmas town on the 10th of December, finished it on the 20th of December, and kept it in operation until the 10th of January. This little wonderland was placed between the Royal Palace and the Cina Restaurant in the Palace Square. So our subject was able to see it, day and night, from her apartment windows. It was one of a child's greatest joys to be allowed by the parents to enter the little town and to check through all of the little cottages and boutiques. There were available various candies, chocolates, toys and a few places where they could buy cotton candy. But the highest attractions of the little town were the places where the children could watch their favorite cartoon characters: Mickey Mouse, Donald Duck. Snow White and the Seven Dwarfs, and the three Little Pigs. Years later, the subject learned that the little town was a scaled-down version of Disneyland with little streets and bridges and cardboard castles, meant to make a child to feel like real character in a fairy land.

Ceausescu Becomes President

Exactly when the world seemed to be a tranquil and well-ordered for her, Gheorghe Gheorghiu-Dej, Romania's first communist president died. She was in the third grade, 10 years old. As she remembers, nothing special happened at that time. There were only three days of mourning and a black sign on the portrait hanging in the classroom. But nobody was crying on the streets and she would call the funeral "rather humble." There were a few rumors about who the future president would be and then suddenly, the most beloved "Son of the People," appeared, the most clever shoemaker-scientist, the one who was greeted by the sun itself.   Nicolae Ceausescu brought black clouds on the serene sky of the country from his first days as Romania's leader. He began to spread the rumor that Gheorghe Gheorghiu-Dej was a weak and worthless president who would not be mentioned in the history books.

Dana could not make any decisions about the new president during the first months, but in December, she definitely decided that he was a cruel beast. Why in December? Because in December, the little "Children's Town" disappeared forever. Ceausescu gave as the reason for eliminating the children's town that due to security rules he could not allow this crowded activity to occur so close to his central committee building. In this action, he killed in cold blood the hopes and joys for thousands and thousands of children in Bucharest.

He also said that the country needed a strong energy saving policy, so he cut off the marvelous fountain we mentioned before and diminished the lighting of the city. At that time, all of the shops had electric signs for advertising. These were extinguished by Ceausescu as he said, "Use painted signs." Where Gheorghiu-Dej tried to cover the ugly face of communism which killed thousand of intellectuals in the early 1950s spending part of the budget for lights, good food, and heat in the apartments, Ceausescu used the same money to build tens of useless industrial dinosaurs and huge villas all over Romania for his own private benefit.

As Dana recalls, Gheorghe Gheorghiu-Dej, was tempted by grandeur too, but he was willing to share the country's riches with the entire population. Gheorghe Gheorghiu- Dej was smart enough, while killing the intellectuals on one hand, to share the country's riches with the population on the other. He didn't build any villas for himself. He wasn't afraid to go and talk to the workers and farmers freely, without security bodyguards, because he was trying to offer some benefits to the population too: free education, free health care, good heat and lights, foreign movies. He didn't start any cult of personality. He still had his CFR (Romanian National Railway) personality and some decency. He made sure that the wonderful Peles Castle (the monarchy's Summer Palace) was kept in good condition as a museum available to anyone at no charge. Our subject was able to visit this castle two times after she became a Young Pioneer.

Gheorghe Gheorghiu-Dej also developed a marvelous place for the young students in the Cotroceni Palace[3] which was renamed by him "The Children's Palace." In the Children's Palace, the students were engaged in many wonderful activities: theater, plays, carnival, group study of chemistry, physics, mathematics, literature, history and geography. The children had access to all of the rooms of the palace.

After Ceausescu decided that his private villas were not enough for him, he took for himself the Peles and Cotroceni palaces and these museums were not available for visits by anyone until after the 1989 revolution. He was a complete egomaniac.

While Gheorghe Gheorghiu-Dej was willing to share the grandeur "communist era" with all of the people, Ceausescu wanted to save everything good and valuable exclusively for himself and the bunch of cruel crooks who surrounded him. Gheorghe Gheorghiu-Dej was trying to demonstrate that communism was a good and useful tool to bring beauty and security in people's lives. One of the good memories from the Gheorghe Gheorghiu-Dej years was seeing the expert gardeners arrange a marvelous park around the Congress Hall. They brought from the mountains, about 12 huge fir trees and replanted them in the corners of the park. It was a magnificent performance as they first dug very deep holes in the ground and then an enormous trailer with the fir trees came and four large cranes erected the trees and placed them into the holes. The view was marvelous. Between the 12 fir trees were lots of ornamental bushes with wonderful flowers. Magnolia trees were planted also. From her apartment window, our subject was able to admire, the wonderful park with the fir trees that appeared to have been there for centuries with the magnolias that were in blossom in April and May, with an ocean of roses of all colors. But Ceausescu wouldn't share anything with the population. He was not interested in the park and he fired the gardeners and left everything in ruin.

When she was 13 years old, Dana definitely knew that the system was wrong and based on lies. She used to spend half of her summer vacations with her grandparents in Braila and half of it with her grandparents in Sighetul-Marmatiei. By then, as we said before, she knew a lot of things about the period between the two world wars and about the monarchy and about King Mihai, but it seemed that nobody could do anything against the new orientation in which the government, instead of trying to serve the population, seemed to be preoccupied with trying to impoverish the people. Gradually, Ceausescu began to develop a strong cult of personality. Emulating the North Korean model, he wanted to develop huge demonstrations. Instead of sending the meritorious students to visit the museums such as the Peles and Cotroceni palaces, he sent the Pioneers to the peasants to help with the harvest. The entire population was supposed to work, work, work for free - patriotic labor.

Concurrently, the life in the schools changed. The toilets were no longer clean, the sanitation installations became deteriorated. Nothing was painted and everything became dull gray in color. Life became, day after day, more dull and meaningless. However, our subject decided she could not change the system, but she could work hard on her high school assignments, make good grades, and be admitted to a university to become a teacher, which seemed to be an appropriate job for a woman.

Notes

1. We have given our subject a fictitious name. Both Dana (pronounced as Americans say "Donna") and Munteanu are common Romanian given and surnames.
2. Author's note: I have seen the building and basin at the end where it is evident that the fountain had once existed. The "nonexistence" of the fountain was the result of economy measures on electricity and more than that, the communist leaders said, "What is the fountain good for? To please the people, but our mission is not to please the people. Shut it down!"
3. The Cotroceni Palace had been the Bucharest residence of Romania's Royal family. Ceausescu lived in a palace in the Primavera area of Bucharest, but he worked very hard to make Cotroceni a place for his personal use. Because of all of the investments and modernization at a very large cost, after the revolution, part of the palace became the Presidential executive offices and more than half is available again as a museum that anyone can visit.

Chapter 4

Case Study, Part 2: Teaching at Petrosani

In 1978, when Dana Munteanu graduated from the faculty at the University of Bucharest with a degree in English and linguistics, she was still visiting her grandparents (except for the priest grandfather, who died in 1969). While she was attending the high school and the university between 1970 and 1978, she noticed that many of her colleagues were looking for ways to escape to foreign countries and several of them were successful. Many of them are now in Germany, the U.S., and Israel. They were saying, we want to be free, we want to have access to good music and good jobs and to be able to travel all over the world and to have good opportunities to develop our personalities."

But our subject was not confident enough to take such a step. She was actually content with her private universe because she used to say, "If I'm not happy with the outdoor environment, then I must do something to have a very satisfactory indoor environment." That meant she began to read more and more books in all fields, including a popular version of Einstein's "Theory of Relativity."

She got married in her third year at the university and gave birth to a son the next year. She didn't actually want to have the child, but under Ceausescu, abortions were illegal. At least 200,000 women died trying to get rid of pregnancies without medical assistance during twenty-five years under Ceausescu.

When Dana graduated, she was assigned to a job as a teacher in the gymnasium (high school) in Petrosani, in the Carpathian mountains 400 kilometers west of Bucharest, far from her family, her child, and her husband. Being so far away, she could only visit her family once a month. For this and other reasons, she was divorced in 1980, but she didn't care very much. She told us she wasn't much involved in terrestrial problems at that time.

When she found herself alone in Petrosani with no friends and relatives, 400 kilometers from Bucharest, Dana was amused and after reading so much science fiction, she felt like an alien paying a visit to this planet. "Why should I have been worried or unhappy," she told us, "I'm just a visitor from another planet." Meanwhile, she was listening as often as possible to the Voice of America and Radio Free Europe. She knew that eventually, everything would change again and history would be back in its normal course.

Suddenly, Ceausescu came forth with another draconian decree, saying that all the probationary employees would lose their homes of record for the one where they were then employed. The intent was to save the decaying socialist economy that could no longer provide jobs for the university graduates.[1]

Dana's Arrival in Petrosani

Going back to Dana's arrival in Petrosani, a city of more than 50,000 inhabitants in the center of the coal mining region of Romania, it was a warm summer evening when she got off the train in the Petrosani station. Then the train left and there she was, all alone, with one piece of paper from the government the *repartitie governmentala*, her work assignment, signed by the Minister of Education. It was her contract for three years to teach English at the gymnasium school in Petrosani. She knew no one or where to go, but she was unexpectedly welcomed nicely by the officials in the train station. She spent the night in the guest accommodations at the train station. But unfortunately, a nice beginning was not necessarily followed by a nice continuation.

The next morning when she went to the school, the principal said, "There must be some mistake. I have no place for you. The position you were sent for has already been filled by a graduate from the University of Cluj who is married and has a house in Petrosani. We have to give the job to her" The administrator called the *Judet* (County) School Inspector in Deva, saying, "Look, I have here two government assignments for the same position, one sent by Cluj, one sent by Bucharest. What am I supposed to do?" The response from Deva was that it was not a Deva concern and should be a Bucharest concern, so the principal called the Ministry in Bucharest. At this point, our subject was rather confused. She knew that if she didn't get this position in Petrosani, she wouldn't get a better position, but probably would get a worse assignment in some forgotten village even further from Bucharest. Life in a village would mean no running water, no refrigerator to preserve food, no toilet in the house, but only a hole in an outhouse at the rear of the courtyard, mud on the roads on rainy days, no TV available, and no phone connections with Bucharest. These conditions were not at all attractive to someone who had lived all of her life in the capital city.

She admitted that it was logical for the lady who was married and had a house in Petrosani to get the position since she was expecting to spend the rest of her life in Petrosani. However, the answer from Bucharest was given in a perfect communist style with no regard for the married lady. "The assignment from Bucharest was emitted one day prior to the assignment from Cluj. In addition, Dana Munteanu's grade average was 9.23 (out of 10), while the lady from Petrosani's average was 9.14. The job is for the person from Bucharest and we will find another job for the lady who graduated from Cluj."

At this development, the lady from Petrosani began to cry desperately. Her parents-in-law were high officials in the mining office in Petrosani so they got on touch with officials in the school inspectorate in Deva. The next action she knew of was that the principal called the teachers together and they jointly determined that they could create a new position for the Cluj graduate. This caused a considerable amount of trouble to everyone. What resulted was that our subject, rather than teaching all English classes, had the responsibility to teach half English classes and the other half was Romanian literature. The Cluj graduate had half of her responsibilities in teaching English and half in French. This required that the teachers who had previously been teaching Romanian literature and grammar as supplemental classes, to lose these supplemental hours and with them, one third of their salaries. The same happened to the teacher who had been teaching supplemental French classes.

With these changes, all the problems had apparently been solved and everybody was expecting for the school year to begin at the 15th of September like always. However, our subject had a personal problem. She spoke with the principal.

"I don't want to bother you with my problems but I need a place to stay. I really don't like the dormitory you offered me in the University Campus." (Petrosani has a university which specializes in mining engineering). "All I need is a trusty family that I can rent a room from." The music teacher offered to help when the principal asked the colleagues if they knew about an available room in a good quality house. At first, it was an exciting and pleasant experience for her to go from one door to another to ask for a room. Unfortunately everybody seemed extremely suspicious and most of the people answered with a categorical "NO!"

."What is going on?" asked our subject. "Is there anything wrong with my appearance?"

"No, nothing is wrong with you, but you can't really blame them. A few years ago anybody would have immediately accepted you into their house, but once the owners rent a room to somebody now they lose it. The lodger has no place to move to and stays forever because he gets a visa from *Militie* (Police) on his ID card . The owner cannot get rid of a lodger no matter how bad his behavior turns out to be. That is because he gets the visa only if the owner signs a rental contract for at least three years, and the police will automatically renew it after that. This situation is created because of the lack of available housing."

"But I am not going to stay here forever. I'll go back to Bucharest as soon as possible and I don't need a temporary visa."

"If you have no visa you can not get the monthly portion of oil and sugar and flour."

"I don't need any oil or sugar or flour. I have no family here and I am not going to cook very much and for what I need I'll bring from Bucharest."

"Why didn't you say this from the beginning. Now it will be a lot more easier to get a good room. I will guarantee for you, that you are not going to the Police for a visa."

And so they almost immediately obtained a very nice room in a splendid courtyard very near the school The location was excellent until the cold weather started and she had no wood to start a fire in her stove. Meanwhile, her mother who was more than a little bit concerned about the incredible adventures her daughter was enjoying in the "Far West" of Romania made all the necessary arrangements to put her in a comfortable apartment owned in Petrosani by a friend who was actually living in Bucharest. The only problem was that the apartment was a little bit far from the school and she had to take the bus for four long stops.

The town was nice, clean, and quiet, the landscape with all the high, tree covered mountains surrounding the town was perfect for a dreamer. However, the food was of a very poor quality and often almost nonexistent. In Bucharest and all over the country the food ration had been installed in 1975 and every year the food problems became worse and worse. All of the women were able in that time to have a very nice "silhouette." The ones who suffered the most were the babies and the little children. No milk, no butter, no cheese, no fruit, no lemons and no oranges, and no vitamins. Instead of spending a little of the all hard currency available on citrus fruits for the children of Romania, the megalomaniac Ceausescu was spending it all on foreign spare parts for his industrial dinosaurs. "How can we have a strong people and a powerful country without the minimum decent quantity of food on the table ?" she questioned herself.

At that time, the underground commerce had started. If one knew somebody working in the "OCL Alimentara" chain then he or she would pay extra money for the products but at least the person and his or her family would not starve. Because of the lack of food, everybody was tempted to accept corruption. Corruption meant more money and more money meant more food. In her view, the mafia that is confronting Romania today was created and specialized during those cruel years of starvation.

Defection of General Pacepa

She interrupted the Case Study here to discuss her recently acquired knowledge of General Pacepa[2] who in exactly 1978 (when our subject was assigned for Petrosani) betrayed Ceausescu and made his escape in The US.

Who was General Mihail Pacepa? The Second Chief of the Foreign Intelligence Service of The Socialist Republic of Romania and the head of all the assigned Romanian agents sent by Ceausescu all over the world. As soon as he touched the American land he made public all the information he could provide about the Romanian network of spies and he described in ample detail

everything that was really going on in Romania and the sufferings
of the Romanian People.[3]

She mentioned General Pacepa here because it will be easier for our
readers to understand the events to come on the case study.

Pacepa's defection to the U.S. left Ceausescu speechless and as
furious as a bull in front of a red cape, as the most 'beloved son of
the people' decided the security surveillance was not strong enough
and the people were far too free to think and act. Starting with 1978
he approximately doubled the number of the security officers and the
number of the informers. The informers were a very dangerous
category of persons who mostly blackmailed citizens to be able to
offer information for free to the security officials: in other words,
they were the Security collaborators.

According to the knowledge of our subject, there was a security
informer for every ten people, thus we can say that in any group of
11 persons, one would be connected to the Security Surveillance
System - a system which was supposed to provide total and complete
security for the beloved and his family and some of his most
important acolytes.

Dana is Compromised

After spending three quiet months in the rustic city of Petrosani
our subject was suddenly called into the principal's office. The
principal herself had a very pale, scared face and although they
were all alone in the room, she whispered in our subject's ear "They
called for you at the Police."

"What ? Why?"

" I don't know but it seems it is important. Please promise me
to try not to show you are irritated, and be as nice and as polite as
possible, then whatever the problem is we will solve it."

Our subject was extremely serene knowing she had not done
anything to bring an offence to the officials, no matter who were they
representing. She calmly left the school, crossed the little park near
the police station, and entered the building. The soldier on duty was
surprised to see a young and modestly dressed lady trying to climb
the stairs to the offices.

"There is no program for the public today."

" I know, but I was invited to come here a few minutes ago."

" Ah," said the soldier and picked up the phone. A few minutes later, she was waiting in a room, noticing the beautiful view from the window. Then a young person, dressed as a civilian entered the room.

"Good morning, Mrs. X." He recognized her without ever meeting her before, and spoke her married name. "Have a seat. Would you care for a coffee?"

"No, thank you," she said, but her mind was working very fast: "This is like being in a movie. Nothing can be real," she thought. "My principal told me to be as polite as possible and I was stupid enough to refuse the coffee. What shall I do now?" Then she corrected herself, "A glass of water would be very good."

" Mineral water?"

" Oh, thank you very much."

" Generally speaking you have a good record. It is too bad you decided to divorce your husband, but you can still be a very good citizen. Now we have this new problem. You have been in Petrosani for more than three months and you haven't asked for a temporary visa. According to the law you were supposed to come for registration with the Police no more than 48 hours after your arrival if you are going to spend more than 3 months here. Am I right?"

" I am sure you are but I thought I needed no visa because I am not going to ask for an apartment here and I don't need the ration."

" I was sure you had good reasons not to come here earlier but a law is a law and it says 48 hours. Do you happen to know what is the law saying about those who don't take it into account?"

"Well, I don't know for sure but there must be a fine to be paid"

"Yes, but I assume you need a clean record for your future jobs in Bucharest. Actually this is not the problem I want to talk to you about. Two weeks ago you started to teach a course in English for beginners, invited by the Director of the Cultural Centre. You have 14 students in the class. We would like for you to ask your students why they decided to study English? It is important to us because all of your students happen to be managers in different companies, and we need all the available information. Do you think you have a method to ask them, discretely, why they want to study English? We don't want to offend anybody. In case you come up with a good material on the subject I can tell the police to consider you are in perfect order with the visa."

"Thank you very much. I was worried about the new decree about the home of record."

"You need not worry about anything as long as you help us."
Our subject left the Police building feeling rather dizzy." This cannot be true," she said. "This simply cannot be the truth! I have just became an informer for the Security Surveillance Service. My God! I am an informer! I had no idea how easy is to be forced to become an informer." She knew things about the security system and about the informers from the University. She had colleagues who told her scary stories about people who had been arrested for telling political jokes at parties.

She decided that it was not going to be too dangerous for her students to answer to such an innocent question as, "Why am I studying English?" Perhaps she would not be doing a dirty job after all. She had also been told to never mention to anyone about her meeting with the security officer. Her story was that she had been called to the Police station to solve her visa problem. When her principal heard this fabrication, she was extremely happy that everything turned out just fine.

The next time our subject again met the English student-managers, she was very embarrassed and felt like a spy, but she found enough strength in herself to tell them, "I have real problems with my young students in the school. They say they are going to become miners and don't need to study English. Can you help me in finding good reasons for them? I want to use you as examples for my students. Can you write on a small piece of paper what made you think it is important to study English? And maybe one of these days, you would accept an invitation to meet my class and to talk to the students. You must think of them as your future colleagues or subordinates." And so they did. The wrote things like:

- As a manager of "X" enterprise, I have a subscriptions to a magazine published in England, I want to be able to read and understand it.
- As a specialist in "Y" field, I have been invited to China to work on a plant site, together with other specialists from Poland and East Germany. The requested language is English.
- Almost everybody on the earth is using English to communicate with foreigners: China, Russia, Bulgaria, Poland, etc. This seems to be the international language for the future.
- You never know when you can bump into an English situation (a gorgeous German blonde lady at the seaside you would want to talk with).

Dana was then able to send to Bucharest the requested information in an pre-addressed envelope she had been given. Soon after, she received a phone call from someone, never identified, with a lot of thanks. She never knew what the consequences of her act were, but she prayed to God that nobody had to suffer a loss or anything more serious. And she prayed and she prayed very hard as her grandmothers taught her to do whenever she found herself in trouble, and the Security officers never called for her again in the rest of her life.

Refurbishing the School's Facilities

One of the specific features of our case study here is that we must travel in time back and forth in order not to lose any of the important details that gathered together will give an explicit picture of a lifetime under a communist system.

Now we are back with our subject during the first days of the beginning of the school year. She had come to Petrosani on the 20th of August and the school started on the 15th of September. After the first four days of confusion in trying to find a place to stay, she was happy with her room and relaxed and took her time to find things about the school. The building was well designed and solid, probably built during the peace period between the two world wars. It was located exactly in the center of the town, opposite the City Hall, near the Police Station, and near the School Inspector Council. Speaking of the School Inspector Council, the principal used to say "Whenever they get tired of drinking their coffee and get bored with doing, nothing they cross the street to give us severe inspections and strongly criticize everything they see. But they never try to help us with anything in case we are in need."

A lot of rumors circulated in the school that worthless teachers had been promoted to be inspectors because they had the right connections to the superior school or Party organizations, e.g. "She was not smart enough to tell a flower from a tree and here she is a chief inspector that comes and yells at me as though I were the moron! " (Teacher of biology complaining about a former colleague promoted on bases other than professional skills).

During those days the summer holiday had not ended. Everybody was working on cleaning the school, doing the necessary repairs, repainting the walls, and other useful things to put the school in good condition for the students. Our subject found out there was no money allocated from the General Inspector Council in Deva for the Council in Petrosani so the Council in Petrosani had no means to help the school which would have been the normal way to fund the improvements.   According to the law, the State, through its institutions had to provide the funds, but by that time the Government decided the schools could and must solve their problems by themselves.

How? At first, students were required to bring used paper (all kinds of paper: newspapers, books, etc.) at least 10 kilograms per student and 10 kilograms of scrap iron per student and the school would get a contract to sell these recyclable materials and make some money. Soon everybody discovered that such actions are very complicated so to simplify matters, the teachers decided to ask the students to bring the equivalent of the recyclable materials in money. Even so, the money was not enough to cover the expenses incurred every summer to fix the school properly for a next year.

At that time, Romanians were always able to find ways to solve their problems until later when the economic conditions became so critical that even if they appealed to the PCR (Communist Party of Romania) nobody could solve anything anymore. As we said, PCR is the abbreviation for the Communist Party of Romania, but at that time, a cruel joke (because it was too realistic) was being circulated. When somebody asked "What is PCR the abbreviation for?" The answer was, "The letters come from *Pile, Cunostinte, Relatii (Pile* means "nepotism," *Cunostinte* means acquaintances, *Relatii* means highly connected with important members of the clique)."

When the summer holiday began, every teacher spoke to the parents of the students in his or her class and told them frankly, " Do you see this class? It is the class where your children will spend another year, so please think of something and come with solutions to repair the desks, the blackboard, the windows, and to paint the walls and to clean the floor with petroleum.". So the parents would go back to their working places and they would eventually steal a little bit of paint and of other things they were necessary to fix the class.

They would even tell everything to their chiefs, "Look, boss, I need few days off and a little paint to do some work in the school where my children are studying."

"Take everything you need and don't worry. I'll cover for you.

If somebody asks about you, I'll tell them I sent you to Craiova to bring some spare parts."

"Oh, boss, I knew you were going to understand and the autumn is near. You remember what good wine and cheese I usually bring from the country. I'll definitely save some for you."

"Sure, sure, we have to understand each other, we all have children don't we?"

The timetable was established, the school was almost refurbished, but there were still a lot of parents or workers sent by the parents to help complete the repairs in every class.

"Are they doing this from a patriotic point of view or they are going to get something in exchange?" asked our subject.

"I am glad you asked," said the principal only few days before the school year started. "They are not going to get anything in exchange. Those times when a parent would bring you a goose or a big piece of cheese to obtain a good grade for his child are forever gone. Now according to the latest indications from 'above' we teachers are no longer allowed to try to discipline our students or give them bad grades and force them to have a reexamination in the autumn. All students, no matter how poor their knowledge is, are from the beginning considered graduates."

"Oh, my, it seems everything has changed since the four years I spent in the University. Only four years ago in the high school, we still were extremely concerned about our grades and were afraid to become repeaters ."

"You are too young, you do not understand a lot of things yet. Things have changed a lot in the last four years so I want you to 'be wise' and to take my advice. In order not to put yourself in a difficult situation don't get angry with the students no matter what they do. Try to act with as much authority, dignity, and prestige as you can, and when you find you are in real trouble, come (without telling anybody anything) to me. And above all, don't ever write a bad grade in the catalogue of the class. It is much more difficult to solve something that is already written in an official document where we are no allowed to make changes than to find a reasonable way to get rid of the problem."

"I find it really difficult to have a good discipline in the class and a good motivation for studying without the power that grades were always able to give to a teacher, but I'll try to find a trick so they will be sensitive to my message."

Of course, not all the teachers of Romania in those times were so enthusiastic about finding a device to convince their students that education is very important for the rest of their lives. That is why most of the teachers just accepted the situation and they themselves lost their own motivation to perform high quality teaching. The situation became more dramatic each year and finally the teachers found themselves in the position of having to bring the tests for the class with the answers to the questions and to write both the test and the answers on the blackboard and to let the students copy them. These false tests were necessary for the teachers to be able to put good grades in the catalogue (grade book) and to show them to the school inspectors. In her estimate, by the year 1978, only one third of the students of Romania were involved in real education and this was due to their families and due to their own options and temperament.

Beginning the School Year

September 15th arrived. The students were in their classrooms and our subject met a bunch of nice and naive children in the class for which she was assigned as a sponsor. They were 12 years old. As a teacher, she could do a lot for these still innocent children. She said to herself " If the grades are no longer the motivation for trying to be a good student than let us invent a game that can bring some kind of motivation." She told the students to sit down and she suddenly asked them, " Do you know who I am?"

"Yes, we know you are our sponsor for the whole school year and you are also our teacher for Romanian literature and for English language too."

"Yes, it is true, so we are going to spend a lot of time together, but I want you to know that I am not only your sponsor. I am also your 'Captain,' for this classroom is not just an ordinary classroom, but a big sailing ship trying to cross the ocean." Our subject was perfectly aware that 12 year old children are still pleased by fairy tales and adventures with ferocious pirates. A child would always like to take part in a play that has a special secret plot which brings a lot of excitement to everyone.

"Our ship just left the shore and it is a real adventure for me to be the captain of a crew I know nothing about and I hope it is going to be a nice challenge for you to show me your talents and skills as soon as possible, because we need to find a first mate to help the captain to keep the ship in the right direction and we need a treasurer to take care of our money and a good ship recorder to be able to write everything that happens on our journey in the big ship's log."

Soon after that, everybody was curious about the secret "halo" that surrounded the 5th grade where our subject was the sponsor. However, the oath of silence that the captain took from the sailors on her ship kept everyone else out of the scenario. The trick worked and the children were enchanted with their teacher.

By that time, all students in the 5th grade were Young Pioneers and the pioneer rules said they were supposed to wear their red scarves every day. Sometimes they would forget to bring the scarves or they would bring them dirty or wrinkled. But all the red scarves on the "ship" were perfect. Why? Because the captain said, "We will never allow anybody to catch us in a wrong position. We are going to have 10 scarves in perfect condition, clean and ironed, in our treasure chest, along with all of the necessary supplies that will keep us well even during the strongest storms on the sea: chalk of all colors, pens, pencils, notebooks, a clean tablecloth for the teacher's desk, and everything we need to be in good condition. If you want to become real seawolves, you must be strong serious, and never betray our oath. We do not have boys and girls on our ship, we have only warriors against pirates. They can attack us any minute. You know who the pirates are! The bad grades. If we take bad grades, it means that we can not make to the 6th grade shore and we are lost in the obscure waters of the Ocean."

Ceausescu's Mania for a Larger Population

Months later, her principal said to her, "I am very happy with the way you are sponsoring your students. It is too bad you are planning to go back to Bucharest so soon," said the principal when she heard about our subject's intention to give up the teaching career in order that she could to go back home. Actually, our subject had been disappointed to learn that the story with the pirates which was good enough for children in the 5th grade, was not good at all for teenagers in the middle of the 6th grade and starting with 14 year old students, almost every kind of soul communication she tried seemed pointless. At this age, most of the girls were already women and the boys were smokers. It was extremely difficult to fight with 40 students in a class to try to bring them to their senses. Our subject felt by the end of the school year that she was just wasting her precious time trying to change the world.

The girls were being encouraged to have intimate relations as soon as they were capable to give birth to a child. Ceausescu wanted more and more children to be born every year so he decided that the former rules should be changed under which a student was expelled if she was involved in a scandalous relation that resulted in pregnancy before she graduated from the 12 the grade. From that point on, pregnant students would receive congratulations. Everything seemed upside down to our subject, so she decided she would give up teaching for the rest of her life. Teaching became like a macabre joke in which the students were not even able to copy the answers for the tests written by the teacher on the blackboard in very big letters. In 1978, education seemed to be a lost cause, with 14 year old pregnant girl students and trivial boy students.

Home Visitations: Ceausescu Crushed a Worker Rebellion

Other various aspects from our subject's experience in Petrosani can bring more information about life under a communist system. One of the duties a sponsor was supposed to accomplish during the school year was called, "Visits at the students homes," to see if they had good conditions for living and working. Our subject had 30 students, but she paid visits to only one third of the families because it was embarrassing. The parents were obligated to accept her in the house, but she felt like a spy who had come to report if the house was clean and tidy and all kinds of other details about the private life of the family. One of the communist leader's purposes was to make sure nothing was private anymore. There was to be no more private life. In life and death, the people belonged to the state.

During these visits, she found out that there had been a rebellion in 1977 in Lupeni, another small mining town near Petrosani. In this rebellion, the miners decided that they could no longer work in the subterranean mines while their families starved because food was no longer available on the market. When an official from the government came to talk to them, they took him prisoner and asked for Ceausescu himself to come and see how badly they working and living conditions are. Instead, Ceausescu sent security and army forces to crush the rebellion.[4] The *securitate* elements arrested the most courageous leaders of the rebellion and executed them, but from that moment, the miners received special treatment. The miners got an increase in wages and more food while working, including a hot meal with soup and meat. The entire Valea Jiului (Jiu Valley, the coal mining area of Romania) benefited with better food for a while.

These conditions prevailed for a few months before she had arrived in Petrosani, but gradually, while she was there, the miners were losing what they had obtained the previous year. It had again become very difficult to find meat, cheese, salami, and all of the other necessary food items in the *alimentara*. At that time, there were rumors that the miners might again fight to regain their rightful rewards. But it was going to be very different this time, since Ceausescu decided after the first rebellion to send armed troops to the mines and security personnél to watch over the miner's activities. Soldiers and security officers, some open and some undercover, plus an informer network prevented the miners from getting organized again, no matter how courageous they were.

The Ceausescu Visit to Petrosani

Dana's last memory from Petrosani concerned a planned visit of Ceausescu to take place on the latter part of August, 1979. The summer of 1979 was a pleasant, holiday time until someone announced that a presidential visit was to take place in August. Everyone went crazy, working from dawn to dusk, painting the buildings and planting flowers in open spaces. Somehow, they were able to find the necessary funds to try to improve the face of the town's main street where the president was expected to walk, surrounded by his guardians, to the stadium, where a large meeting would take place.

"This is a false image. Why don't we leave the town as it is, without flowers and fresh paint. Why should we look happy and rich when we are sad and worried about the future?" asked our subject of the principal, who was frantically calling parents to get more students back from their summer holiday to have them to march in the parade.

"Be glad we go through this so rarely. What if we were somewhere in the field and we would have worked to harvest the crops all summer long? Here in the mountains, we can usually enjoy our summer holidays."

Then about ten days before the expected crucial visit, another news bomb was dropped: "The president is not coming anymore." This news, after all of the rehearsals for the parade and the tens of hours of "patriotic work" (work without pay) on the town and the main street and on the stadium! All work stopped at once, leaving some buildings half painted, half unpainted.

It is strange that Ceausescu was able to develop such a cult of personality while everyone was sick of it and hated it, including the communist leaders who encouraged him to show his disdain for his suffering people. Even more strange was how it was possible, year after year starting with 1979, that the population became poorer while the parades became bigger and more extravagant. These are some of the reasons why gradually, everybody started to hate Ceausescu, the man, for his foolish vanity where he was trying to show that he was "The most beloved son of the nation."

"At the end, even his closest collaborators strongly hated him and decided, with no regrets, to shoot him and his wife like dogs. Nobody actually knows where their bodies are buried, because they were lost after the executions at the airport," she added.

Although these last ideas are only rumors, they show the deep disdain of the Romanian people who wanted to get rid of this diabolic dictator as soon as possible. He went from being Chief of State to dying like a tramp dog or a homeless vagrant pushed into an unknown grave without any burial ceremony.

Notes

1.   This decree was abolished after two years because it affected the children of *securitate* as well as other university graduates, so the *nomenclatrua* convinced Ceausescu to rescind the decree.

2.   We referred to General Pacepa and his book, *Red Horizons: ...* in chapter 2.

3.   Her knowledge was from a series of articles in the newspaper *Ziua* about General Pacepa, including excerpts from *Red Horizons*, plus remembrances of discussions about Pacepa broadcast by Radio Free Europe in the years before the Romanian Revolution.

4.   This incident is described in Georgescu, *The Romanians: A History*, 1991, p. 445, and also by Campeanu, p. 2.

Chapter 5

Case Study, Part 3: Return to Bucharest

Early in Dana Munteanu's time in Petrosani, there was still the belief that the decree which would permanently change each Romanian's home of record to where they were currently working would be fully implemented. After the first three months, she started to research the situation to find a way to escape back to her home. For her, as for many other Romanians, Bucharest is the perfect place to live. "If your home is Bucharest, you have the feeling that you are alive, in the center of events, in the middle of the news as it is happening. Suppose Leonid Brezhnev would come to Romania some day? The people of Bucharest would be the only ones to see the Father of Communist Fathers."

Her parents decided to help her. Here, we have an example of how the communist chain of influence was functioning. Our subject's father was an important prosecutor working directly with the General Prosecutor of Romania. He had been a very good subordinate for more than 20 years. Having a good record of party loyalty and service, he went one day in late 1978 to his boss, the General Prosecutor, and said, "My daughter is getting a divorce and she is in danger of losing her house and child in Bucharest because her job is far from Bucharest in Petrosani. I would like to bring her to Bucharest."

"She has good reasons to come back home," said the General Prosecutor.

"Yes, but the Minister of Education didn't approve her *memorium* (petition)."

No matter how valid and correct a persons reasons for transfer might be, no one could obtain a transfer without powerful connections at the highest levels. With the help of her father's boss, she finally got the approval to give up teaching in Petrosani, but it was then difficult to find a suitable job in Bucharest.

Finding Employment in Bucharest

She spent six months trying to find a job that would use her English skills, such as that of a librarian who would handle English publications. It seemed that in 1979, a lack of jobs for intellectuals had already been established. When a student graduated from a university, unless he or she was an engineer, the new graduate had better stay in his or her assigned position, because there was no market for educated individuals. The government ministries could force any organization to take a new graduate, but nobody would offer a job to unemployed graduates.

At the end of March, 1980, her mother by chance met Anca, a former colleague from the Academy of Economic Studies, who was at that time the Secretary of the Communist Party Organization for the Light Industry Ministry. Anca's organization controlled the *Centrale* (Centrals), which were the subordinate organizations that controlled several factories in the same industry. For example, a factory producing shoes would be subordinated to the Leather Industry Central which also controlled all other Romanian factories that produced shoes. The Leather Industry Central, combined with the Ready Made Clothes Central, Cotton Industry Central, and several others made up the Light Industry Ministry.

Anca of the Light Industry Ministry soon after met an old friend who was the Chief of the Planning Department of the Glass and Porcelain Central. She told him that if he would help her by getting a job for her friend's daughter, she would help him to get his planning figures accepted. Since each of the centrals had at least twenty factories under its control, this request did not seem difficult. This Chief of Planning for Glass and Porcelain Central created a job for our subject in the Bucharest Fiber Glass Factory.

The truth of the matter was that there was no job there, but a higher level 'planner,' in charge of production figures, could increase the required output and make operations very difficult for a factory director, so there was not likely to be opposition to a job placement when the central's planner said to place someone. Overnight, instead of one training officer, there were two training officers assigned to the factory. Two training officers in a factory of only 1,500 employees looked like a miracle, but any miracle was possible for a strong person in the communist chain of influence. It was possible because two secretaries of the communist party were, at the same time, chiefs of planning departments, one in the ministry which was able to change employment figures and one at the central level who was forceful enough to make the change.

When she presented herself at the factory, a new complex of buildings that had been in operation for only one year, our subject was greeted with disbelief and shock by the factory director when she handed him her authorization papers. She said, "I have been sent by the central."

He answered, "Yes, yes, but it is probably for a few months, because we don't need two people for the same job. But actually, I don't care. The central gives the job and it gives the money to pay your salary too."

It turned out to be not for a few months, but eleven years. What happened? Somebody at a higher level checked on the background of the other training officer. She had never been married, had no children, and was half Jewish with relatives in Israel and Austria - a real danger for the communist system, except for the fact that she was the niece of the Supply Director in the Light Industry Ministry.

Anca, the Secretary of the Communist Party in the Light Industry Ministry who arranged for the job told this story later. "The Supply Director came one day to see me. "What can we do? My niece and your niece (she had recommended our subject as her 'niece') are fighting for the same job. I am a Director while you are only the Chief of the Planning Department, but you are also the Secretary of the Communist Party in the Ministry. I have 'executive power' while you have political power."

"OK, let's combine these powers and we will go together to the minister himself. We will convince him that we need a sociologist training job in the factory for your niece."

And so they did and the minister approved the additional job. Our subject later became a good friend with the sociologist. (Both were the same age.)

Even the inspectors from the central were surprised to find a sociologist assigned to such a small factory. Other important plants and institutes had not been recommended to have such a sophisticated job and here where no special training was necessary for the work, a sociologist was added? Of course as long as the two people in the ministry had their important positions, nobody would challenge the arrangement.

At this point, everything seemed perfect for Dana. The only unpleasant problem was the distance between the factory and her house, 21 kilometers! With three different means of transportation, she could cover the distance every morning, hanging sometimes heroically on the bus door, often destroying her clothing in the process. The difference between men and women had been killed long before, and men no longer felt the inclination to be protective and polite. On the contrary, men under communism in Romania were ready to say bad words to women, no matter what age. This was in retaliation for the equality in the workplace enforced by the communist system. So after one hour spent in three crowded, foul smelling buses, our subject was "happily" starting her work day to do nothing. In the three month period while the ministry was approving the sociologist job, nobody gave our subject anything to do. Her connection in the central told her not to worry. "You must be at work on time, and do not leave early. You must not ask for any time off during the workday 'till we solve the problem. We must show everybody that you are a good quality employee. You come in on time, you leave at the appropriate time. You are humble, you do not ask for any favors, and use this time to find out things about the factory."

Finally, among very suspicious office mates (most found out that she was the daughter of a prosecutor which made her, *inter alia*, an informer) she was able to find a few friendly people. She asked details about the organizational structure because she wanted to integrate herself into the factory quickly. In doing so, she learned that British specialists were still there trying to teach the Romanians how to work the newest section. It had been completely outfitted with equipment from France, Switzerland, and England. She very soon heard the rumor that this Romanian factory was using three times as many workers as the British would use to produce the same quantity of products.

Recruiting Workers

Since she was friendly and talkative, she soon made friends among the workers in the sections and among the engineers and many other employees of the factory. Fiber glass production was something new for the Romanians. Everybody was saying, "We are a 'special objective' (Special Project). We work for the army and other Romanian customers."

However, the working conditions were very, very difficult. Near the hot fibers coming from the glass melting ovens, the temperature was almost unbearable because there was not a good ventilation system as would be found in Britain. Under the *filieare* where the workers were washing the fibers with water, the workers feet were always wet and they caught colds easily. All over the place, fiber glass particles floated through the air, covering everything and going into everyone's nostrils. The factory doctor said the fibers were not harmful, but the Institute for Work Protection was always concerned and provided the best creams and materials to avoid industrial diseases. Even so, the worker turnover rate was very high: if the factory hired 100 employees in a month for this section, only 20 would get accustomed to the conditions and stay a longer time.[1]

There were three sections where the work was very difficult: the glass melting section with its high temperatures, the fiber twisting section with very high speed equipment and a lot of noise, and the sewing section, again with a lot of noise. One of her first discoveries was that nobody from Bucharest would accept to work in any of these sections because of these conditions. However, there was a need for 400 workers in these sections. Soon after she was designated as Training Officer for the factory, her boss told her, "Since no one from Bucharest is applying for work here, we have received approval from the *Centrale* to bring tenth grade graduates, averaging seventeen years old, from Moldova to qualify them here in short courses. You must go to the glass factory in Suceava and spend one week or more to bring workers."

The young people from Suceava were mostly peasants, knowing nothing about city life. There were no jobs for them in the Moldova area. In 1978, it seems that industrial development virtually stopped all over the country. All of the big impressive plants were built between 1950 and 1975, then there was no more money for investment and development. For this reason, and the very high birth rate in this area, Suceava and other Moldavian counties had no jobs for young people.

Our subject made about six trips to Moldova and brought about 1000 workers in one year, but only 300 stayed with the factory due to homesickness and the poor working conditions. After this year, the *Scoala Profesionala* (Apprentice School) started providing 120 trained workers each year to replace the worker turnover.

The new workers from all sources were put into the factory dormitory, four to a room, with four beds, a sink, with toilets, and showers on the common corridor. Very soon, bad news came from the dormitory. The toilets were stopped up and the workers were using the floor for their toilet needs. The rooms were extremely dirty. Since these workers were independent persons earning salaries, they were expected to make sure their rooms were clean and in good repair, but due to their lack of education and culture, they preferred to pay for damages rather than trying to keep everything clean and in repair. The result was that everything was dirty and greasy, with a lot of cockroaches, rats and mice, and broken facilities. The notion of self respect and respect for others had disappeared over the previous twenty years.

Our subject was horrified over what she could see in the girl's dormitory - the filth was sometimes worse than in the boy's dormitory. She told her boss, "We must do something. We must try to educate them, because they are like savages." She tried to speak to the girls a few times and she told them how nice and comfortable it would be to return from the factory each day to a nice, clean place. But, it was in vain. Looking at these eighteen year old girls, our subject, who by was in her early thirties, became extremely worried about the new generation which would rule over the country in the future.

Political versus Administrative Control

In the factory, every step taken was an example of life under a communist system. We would probably need 100 pages to describe all of the details. There was a complex of "confused ownership." The factory was under double control like all enterprises in the country. The whole economy was based on a strongly centralized system, both from the administrative and the political point of view.

1. Political control was exercised by the Party Sector Committee (Bucharest was divided into six sectors) and by the Capital Communist Party Committee. Political control was meant to provide guidance in obtaining the best results in productivity and also to closely watch over the political level of the workers. The instructors from the PCR were in charge of checking on the results

of the "Great Socialist Competition" developed between the organizations located in the same sector. The communist leaders were aware that without a sense of competition, there could not be a strong economy, or at least a satisfactory economy to cover the internal needs. "So, they invented the Great Socialist Competition. Being created on a false basis, it was just another big and useless communist lie that only brought more bureaucracy into people's lives and no rewards." Dana questioned, "How can you have a real competition between forty-seven organizations of totally different profiles, activities and services simply because they were located in the same sector under the same PCR Committee control? This stupid mixture meant to be an impulse in working harder and better produced only more papers in the PCR statistics department."

The political control was concerned, especially for the last five years before the revolution, with the political level of all of the employees, workers and administrators. There was a communist party organization for the entire factory and for all of the sections and sub-sections. Heading the factory's communist organization, there was a Communist Party Secretary meant to be as powerful as the factory's general manager. Actually, the communist secretary had no power concerning the productive activity of the factory. The secretary could not propose or discuss the planning figures, suppliers, or buyers. He or she was more concerned with the discipline and ideological activity. The ideological activity consisted of meetings every month in which the employees were supposed to debate on certain subjects recommended by the Party Sector Committee.

2. Administrative control: exercised by a) the Glass and Porcelain Central b) the Light Industry Ministry. The Central and the Ministry were trying very hard to keep production figures high. While the Political Control would come with new suggestions that could actually kill the production, the Administrative Control had to fight back at the highest levels to avoid the death of the factory. The PCR would suddenly decide: "Strong restriction on electrical power. For a few hours a day there will be no electricity for certain sections of the factory. Part of the equipment will have to be turned off." The *Centrala* would respond: "You do not understand! There are glass melting ovens in the fiber glass factory. If we turn them off for only thirty minutes, we lose the ovens because the liquid glass will solidify and break the ovens and it will cost billions of lei to replace

them."

The PCR would reply: "Then find other solutions: reduce lights in the sections, in the offices, do not heat the building during the winter."

Centrala: "Then what about the workers?"

PCR: "Tell them to wear more sweaters."

Everyday, someone from PCR Committee Number 6 or from PCR Committee Capital or from the central or from the ministry controlled (inspected) the factory's activities. The controllers always showed their dissatisfaction: the quality of the products was not good or the quality of the ideological level was not high enough. Our subject was able to hear the rumors after these daily controls. The factory secretary of the communist party and the general manager were in real trouble.

One or the other would say, "We can punish them (the workers) every day, but they are not going to work any better. Imagine that you are one of them. You have a small salary, no food available, a few crowded busses to take you to the factory and back home. We have come to the point where our employees and workers have no motivation at all On the contrary, we need them and we need to cover for them."

At this point in 1987, our subject was politically promoted to be the second in command of the factory's union. The "union" was not truly representing the worker's interests, but was another method of control on them. Dana was selected for this position due to her writing ability gained from graduating from the Romanian Literature Faculty at the University of Bucharest. She was greatly appreciated for her rapid writing of the materials needed to be shown as proof of the political activity developed by the union and the PCR organization.

When an inspector from the *Centrala* or from the Party Committee was coming the general manager and the secretary would say, "We have no problems with our employees and workers. They are in time for work, we have good discipline. They pay their party dues, they buy the recommended newspapers. They try to do their best in spite of the fact that the raw materials are not of good quality. But, we would like to ask for your help. Try to talk to the Minister of Transportation to increase the number of buses on this route because this factory is far from the town and it is difficult for the workers to walk this distance (about three miles) and we don't want them to be tired already when they start the new work day." However, the central and the communist party secretary were not able to help because the Ministry for Transportation belonged to the army and nobody could interfere with its decisions.

On several occasions, the general manager and the factory's communist party secretary plus representatives from the central and higher level communist organizations went to see the Minister of Transportation.   On one of these occasions, the Minister of Transportation said, "I have this problem all over Bucharest, but I don't have enough buses and enough spare parts to increase the service for anybody." The factory manager then asked him for a letter saying that the number of busses couldn't be increased even though there was a need for them.   From that point on, when an inspector came to the factory and complained that workers were arriving late, the general manager would produce the letter for the inspector to see, and that was the end of the complaint.

Accommodation Within the Factory

From time to time, news from the Communist Party Counsel Sector 6 would come:

"Your factory must provide 400 workers for the meeting concerning international peace problems where the president himself is going to give a speech. You must carry 40 portraits, 25 of the President and 15 with Comrade Elena Ceausescu." (These portraits were fairly large and heavy, nicely framed, and the factory paid for them and the communist party and kept them in a special warehouse for such occasions.)

"We need 400 workers to work in the new park to plant trees and to remove large stones."

"We need 200 workers to sweep the streets. (Every factory was required to help in these activities.) 20 of them each Sunday to cover the next ten Sundays."

"We need 400 workers to help the CAP (*Cooperativa Agricola de Productie*) with sorting the potatoes and the onions."

The general manager would say to the secretary of the communist party, "They need, they need, they need. They need to take our workers for free from production every week, but they are not able to help us with any of our problems. They couldn't do anything about the transport to improve it. They couldn't solve the problem of our cantina to bring warm food and soup for the workers, and they couldn't help us with the food shop. I told them, 'I have more than 900 women workers. They are married and have children. They cannot concentrate on working well because they become too worried about the food they are supposed to provide for their children. Help me with a little shop in the factory, only for my women workers and bring a certain ration of meat, cheese and cold cuts per month per person.' It was only 900 persons involved, but I've been asking for this shop for more than 4 years and nobody will help me. This is a bad sign. A bad sign saying that the nice story about the happy life under communism is just a big lie."

More than that, instead of doing something for the workers about the food problem and the transportation problem, the communist party decided to send a gynecologist every month to every factory to check every woman between the ages of 16 and 41 to see if they were pregnant and more specifically to register them so they wouldn't dare to get an illegal abortion. So, every month, the women were forced to come to the doctor like slaves or like cows to spread their legs on the table to be checked. This was extremely offensive to everybody. Women felt that they were no longer entitled to have their intimacy and their privacy.[2]

Meanwhile, at least one woman in sector 6 would die every month while desperately trying to get rid of her pregnancy. The dead young woman would be leaving behind three other children and a confused, drunkard husband. A veil of tragedy was covering the country. A lot of desperate parents, losing their daughters, and desperate widowers would curse Ceausescu openly. But Ceausescu wanted more and more children. What for? To keep them in freezing apartments with no heat during the winter? With no food and no decent living conditions? Nobody ever found out the reasons except for a megalomaniacal desire to be the president of a growing country.

When the health minister tried to tell Ceausescu, "There is not enough heat in the hospitals during the winter so that the doctors can take good care of little babies and mothers," Ceausescu fired him. Nor could Ceausescu provide food and jobs for these thousands of children. Yet, if a woman was saved from a cruel death caused by an attempt at an illegal abortion, the authorities would immediately put her in jail.

Right after Brezhnev died in 1983, the factory's general

manager, being perfectly aware of what was going on with the communist system, decided together with the secretary of the communist party to cover and to lie about everything. "Our workers spend one hour to come to work, then they spend eight hours in our difficult working conditions, then they spend another hour to go back home and probably a few hours trying to find something to eat. I'm not going to force them to spend other useless hours in the factory pretending they are studying the communist party materials. We are going to tell everybody that all of the planned meetings are taking place." The party activists knew they were being deceived, but they didn't care. In their turn, they also lied in their reports.

Dissatisfaction in all Aspects of Life

Everybody was trying to maintain a semblance of normal life under adverse conditions, but they felt that a revolution was going to take place. The population had no other alternatives. In addition to standing in long lines for the meager food available, many other deprivations became worse during each year of their lives. In the late 1980's in Bucharest, the largest city with almost two million people, and all of the other large cities:

-The electricity was turned off for at least four hours each day, with at least two of those hours in the evenings so nobody could read or write, children couldn't do their homework. This was true in the hospitals as well as in the apartments. This existed for the last three years before the revolution.

-There was hot running water only two hours each day.

-There was television only 2 hours a day, with only one channel, generally showing what Comrades Nicolae and Elena had done for the Romanian people that day.

-There was not enough gasoline for automobiles.

-Historical areas of Bucharest were destroyed to make room for Ceausescu's grandiose building projects which completely changed the Unirii area and had the Casa Poporului in progress when the revolution occurred.

-Ceausescu said, "The Romanian people eat too much." He also determined that too much energy was being wasted by each family cooking meals in their own kitchens, so he was having "food factories" built in Bucharest to make the population eat their meals in these centralized facilities. The revolution occurred and he and his wife were killed before the food factories were completed.

The End of That Ordeal

Though she didn't exactly know what democracy was, our subject knew it had to be ten thousand times better for the people than communism. When the Revolution began in Timisoara in December, 1989, being a union leader, she had been told to go with her factory's workers to Independence Square to listen to President Ceausescu denounce the hooligans who were fomenting trouble for the glorious communist paradise in Romania. Instead of hearing Ceausescu taking charge of the situation, she heard him being denounced and vilified by the crowd. Radio Free Europe and the Voice of America had told of women and children who had been shot down in Timisoara. The mood of the crowd was angry; the people had suffered enough from this tyrant.

Confused and frightened, Ceausescu tried to recapture the crowd (at Elena Ceausescu's suggestion), by promising pay raises. This effort only brought more cat calls and denunciations which the securitate men in the crowd ignored. The crowd which became a screaming mob surged toward the Central Party Headquarters where Ceausescu stood. Ceausescu faded back into the building, never to be seen in public again.

The people took over Bucharest. It was one of the happiest days of our subject's life.

Notes

1.   I have visited factories in Bucharest in 1992 that seemed very unhealthy and even unsafe for workers. In one factory, we passed near a section were two women without ear protection were cutting pieces from a steel bar about 4 inches square. The cutting device made an extremely loud noise as it cut the metal. The metal cuttings were then heated in a furnace and when red hot, were taken out with tongs and thrown across the room to a crew of men who dodged out of the way of the red hot metal, then picked them up and placed them into a shaping press which pounded them several times, with sparks flying everywhere, into a spherical shape, ultimately to become huge ball bearings.
2.   Gallagher states, "Henceforth there was no corner of society in which the state could not interfere. Thus, in 1986, Ceausescu proclaimed the foetus 'the socialist property of the whole society. Giving birth is a patriotic duty.'" Gallagher, pp. 61-62.

Chapter 6
Aftermath of Revolution

There is much speculation about whether there was complicity in the revolution which some writers call a "palace coup."[1] Interestingly, a group of 180 former Ceausescu fellow travelers, calling themselves the National Salvation Front (NSF) were organized and ready to take control of the government at the time it began. On December 21, 1989, the leader of the NSF, Ion Iliescu, telephoned Mihail Gorbachev in the Soviet Union to tell him. "I am in control here." Iliescu and Gorbachev had studied together at the Frunze Military Academy in Moscow. In the 1950's, Iliescu had been a leader in the Young Communist League which terrorized the students at the University of Bucharest where he was a student. His ruthless persecution of "unreliable students" marked him for fast elevation in the Romanian Communist Party RCP) activities.[2] He had supported Ceausescu in the 1960's, but had lost favor with the dictator in 1971 for what was called "intellectualism."[3] After his removal from Ceausescu's inner circle, he had been relegated to minor Romanian Communist Party activities in Timis County and later directed a technical publishing house in Iasi, where he apparently bided his time, but made connections to form an opposition movement against Ceausescu when the time was right.

National Salvation Front Comes Forward
The newspaper, *Scanteia Poporului* announced in a front page article on December 23, 1989, that the forces which had toppled the Ceausescu government had "declared firmly for socialism, for the people's ownership and honest socialist principles untinged by the adventurist spirit and political demagogy of the Ceausescu clan."[4] Thus it appeared that the NSF under Iliescu was going to embark on

a form of *perestroika* (restructuring) similar to that undertaken by Gorbachev. Iliescu, though not a Stalinist type of communist, was far from being anti-communist. Georgescu tells us that Iliescu told a group of students in 1990 that political pluralism was, "an outmoded ideology of the nineteenth century."[5] Thus he did not want a "loyal opposition" in his government.

Many Romanians were then outraged at the program of the NSF. They felt that the revolution to eliminate communism had been stolen from them and a new form of communism would replace the old. Pro-democracy advocates rose up in protest. A statement named the "Timisoara Proclamation," in honor of the freedom fighters who started the revolution, became the platform of the anti NSF forces. In this proclamation, it was made clear that the revolution had been anti-communist as well as anti-Ceausescu and former communists should be banned from public office for three consecutive legislatures after the revolution.[6]

Rather than achieving this goal, the pro-democracy advocates were given the shock in late January, 1990, of learning that the NSF was converting into a political party and would be running in elections scheduled for May of that year. Numerous parties (more than 80) had been created by that time and due to opposition pressure, the NSF agreed to share power, pending elections, with the opposition in a 253 member Provisional National Unity Council, but the NSF and its supporters occupied 111 seats on the council while Iliescu and his NSF dominated provisional government controlled day to day activities.

As the time for the elections approached, there were mass demonstrations daily in Bucharest. There was a fifty-four day sit-in demonstration made up of students, workers, and intellectuals against the Iliescu provisional government at the University Square demanding the government's resignation.[7] The protesters also wanted an independent television station to present a side to the news in addition to that being broadcast by the NSF. To publicize this demand, "On April 22, 1990, a large demonstration marched on the television station, calling for Iliescu's resignation. In a sudden predawn raid, riot police attacked and beat the demonstrators who had spent the night in the University Square...Iliescu denounced the demonstrators as *golani* (bums). It was a shocking word. *Golani* was how Ceausescu had described the demonstrators in Timisoara," at the beginning of the revolution in 1989.[8]

Marcel Cornis-Pope evaluated the election strategy of the NSF as follows, "Iliescu's National Salvation Front presented itself as an original alternative to the multi-party system... But this philosophic argument against genuine political pluralism has worn thin...In the 1990 elections, NSF capitalized on the ingrained paternalism, xenophobia, and anti-intellectualism of ordinary people especially in the rural areas"[9] and won the election easily, although there were allegations of election irregularities confirmed by international observers. Iliescu "received" 85 percent of the presidential votes and his NSF party placed 263 members into the 385 seat Chamber of Deputies and 91 into the 119 member Senate.[10]

The sit-in at University Square continued beyond the elections of May, 1990. It was ultimately broken up using excessive force in June, 1990, by police backed by illegally armed miners from the Jiu Valley who had been called in by Iliescu and who were publicly thanked by him for their support. The violence of this action brought revulsion from around the world and negated much of the sympathy Romania had received since the overthrow of Ceausescu.

The National Salvation Front's Government

The NSF government was put together by interim Prime Minister Petre Roman who had been educated in western Europe and was a professor at Bucharest Polytechnic Institute.[11] Roman appeared to have some workable ideas for reform. He wanted to restructure the national economy on the criteria of profitability and efficiency and to eliminate central direction of the economy. In a January 4, 1990 speech, Roman reported that as a result of the policies of the previous regime, the Romanian economy was in a profound crisis and that the government's first priority would be to get the economy out of the crisis state and to start meeting the immediate needs of the people. The NSF leaders were troubled by the low productivity in the economy, a state that was partially due to shortfalls in energy and raw materials. Other factors that were believed to contribute to the low productivity: poor work habits and labor unrest.[12]

Initially, decrees were promulgated which gave back to the people the right to own private property and to form private businesses. After the May 20, 1990 election in which Iliescu won the presidency and the NSF won 67 percent of the seats in parliament,

Roman moved quickly to begin more sweeping economic reforms. Early laws supposedly took the oversight of state owned enterprises away from the central government and created local boards of directors for each enterprise. The realities, however, differed from the supposed intent, and the boards of directors still presented almost all decisions to their parent government ministries and would take few actions without ministry approval.

Fulbrighters to the Rescue

More than one year later, September, 1991 my group of Fulbrighters came to Romania to see how the transition was progressing and to assist if we could.[13]   Only one month before, an attempted coup in the USSR riveted our attention. What would it mean if the hard liners in Moscow deposed Mihail Gorbachev and returned to the bad old days of stringent confrontation against the West?   Fortunately, we did not have to find out the answer to that question because the coup failed and Boris Yeltsin became the strongest individual in the Soviet Union, which was soon to dissolve. However, the plotters, the "gang of eight" had thought they had all of the forces lined up to overthrow Gorbachev and *perestroika*. What they were lacking was the people of Russia and their President, Boris Yeltsin who refused to cave in to this pressure to turn back to repression and cold war. Unexpectedly to the plotters, the Russian people did not accept this attempt to destroy the fledgling democratic movement.

Vladimir Posner, the Russian television personality that we saw frequently on American television in the years 1985 to 1991, wrote a documentary of the attempted coup in *Eyewitness: A Personal Account of the Unraveling of the Soviet Union*.[14]   It was frightening at the time to think that the cold war would begin again, but we have to feel good that the Russian people did not allow it to happen. The hard liners would have returned the Soviet Union to the old ways of repression and confrontation, something we neophyte Fulbrighters feared because of Romania's close proximity to the USSR. The coup attempt was old news and virtually forgotten by the time we arrived in mid-September, 1991.

In our orientation at the American Cultural Center in Bucharest, we were welcomed by Ambassador 'Punch' Green who told us that he liked Prime Minister Roman's economic restructuring and felt that it held great promise for improvement in Romania's economy. The American Embassy's political officer, Brian Flora, said that the Iliescu government was still popular with older Romanians, but many of the younger Romanians were dissatisfied with the lack of progress achieved by the NSF. Among opposition parties, the Civic Alliance was growing in popularity, but he felt that Iliescu would get 55 percent of the vote if an election were held at that time. He felt that most Romanians wanted peace and stability rather than revolutionary change. The finishing touches on a new constitution (approved by 77 percent of the voters in December, 1991) was occurring at that time. The new constitution allowed the multi-party system and free market practices, but excluded the possibility of a return to monarchy government.

George Flowers, the embassy's economics officer then told us that per capita income of Romania was $1,200 - a figure that equaled the per capita income in Sri Lanka or any one of several Latin American countries. He felt that the figure was not realistic when the educational level, national resources, and capacity for industrial output were compared with these "poor" countries. In 1991, industrial output was 40 percent lower than in 1989. Romania was no longer selling tractors, freight cars, locomotives, and railroad rails to Comecon, the economic organization of the former Soviet block. Romanian producers were looking to the west for selling its products, but were not very successful at that time.

Flowers stated that when Ceausescu had paid off all foreign dept in the last years of his regime the payoff hit his citizens doubly hard. Not only had he exported food and consumer goods away from the Romanian people, but he had also eliminated Romania's foreign debt, a factor that was motivating western nations to support the Czech Republic, Poland, and Hungary after 1989, so that these nations would be able to pay their debts.

Romania's law for privatizing state owned enterprises, authored by western consultants and pushed through the parliament by Petre Roman, had been enacted in August, 1991, just the previous month. It called for certificates of ownership to be given to all 18 year olds and older which indicated that they in the aggregate owned 30 percent of the value of 6,000 state owned enterprises. A "State Ownership Fund" owned the other 70 percent and was charged with selling its ownership in the individual companies so that they would become private.[15]

Thirty large enterprises were to be privatized by the end of 1991, Flowers told us. Five "private ownership funds" were to be created to manage the 30 percent of the value of the state owned companies for the "stockholders" (the Romanian people, sixteen years of age and older) while the State Ownership Fund was selling off its ownership of the other 70 percent. In the next eleven months, while we were in Romania, not one large enterprise was made private, and by the end of 1992, only two: Ursus Brewery and Vranco Knitwear, became private.

Many problems occurred on the road to privatization. For example, the government could not agree on ways to evaluate the worth of the state enterprises. And while most plant managers said that they wanted to be privatized, many were actually obstructionist when the process was aimed at their enterprise. Most of these enterprises were managed by engineers. Economics Officer Flowers told us that the highest priority for general managers was still toward maintaining a high level of employment. If they didn't, they feared that workers would turn on them and actually cause bodily harm to them. The second highest priority was to keep salaries up and the third was to keep good contacts with the government. Nowhere was there any concern for efficiency or high quality. Many of the enterprises employed two to three times as many employees as were needed for efficient operations.

On the bright side in the economy was the figure that showed 150,000 new business startups since the revolution. Entrepreneurship had come to life in this land where there had been no privately owned businesses before 1989. Most of these privately owned businesses were very small, often only a man and his wife running a small shop, or one or two people operating a one car taxi business.

Romanian speakers at the orientation said that the economy was still a "socialist" economy. The government's actions seemed to be toward retaining as much centralization as possible and maintaining many monopolies. The government still set prices for goods and restricted sellers at any level from making more than 30 percent profit on merchandise.

Some land reform was occurring, but the Romanian speakers called it a "fake" land reform. The government was giving small parcels of land back to original owners but without land titles. Many of the new owners then lived in the cities and had no interest in going back to becoming farmers.

Early Excitement

In the same week as our arrival in Bucharest, the miners from the Jiu Valley also came to Bucharest. They fought pitched battles up and down Boulevard Magheru and its continuation, Strada Balcescu, between University Square (*Piata Universitate*) and Romania Square (*Piata Romana*). Ostensibly, they were trying to increase their wages, but there was much evidence to indicate that they had again come at the behest of President Iliescu to show to the people that the Petre Roman reforms were going too rapidly and should be curtailed. The major result was that Petre Roman resigned from the position of Prime Minister and was replaced by a technocrat, the former Finance Minister, Theodor Stolojahn. Stolojahn did not have as much enthusiasm for reform as had Roman, thus many reform programs such as the privatization program stalled. This seems to have been the wish of Iliescu, who apparently felt that he was losing control of the country.

Our Work as Educators

As we Fulbrighters went forth to our teaching or consulting duties, we soon faced the grim realities of trying to influence an established bureaucracy. The professors in the Romanian universities had been teaching certain ideas and using outmoded teaching methods, but they didn't want to change. In most classes, only the professor had a textbook and he or she would read from that textbook while the students took copious notes on everything that was read to them. Students on average were in class 30 hours per week compared to 20 hours per week for western students. "Out of class" assignments were rarely given by Romanian professors, except in the last year of study when a large project was to be accomplished. Western professors routinely give many "out of class" assignments throughout a school term as a method of developing self learning and initiative. We wanted to use this education technique in Romania to ascertain how much independent thinking was possible by Romanian students.

To facilitate the learning process, we Fulbright professors wanted to get some textbooks we had brought from the U.S. into the hands of our students so that we could give them reading assignments and "out of class" assignments. In trying to initiate this activity, we met with a lot of opposition. The books we brought were secreted away in a "Research Library" and the students would have to go there to read them. Only with some embassy assistance, were we able, after some weeks, to get the books into the hands of the students. In the Winter semester, we found that we had to fight the same battle over again. The university administrators did not want to allow students to have textbooks for home use.

Once we had textbooks in the students' hands, we had them reporting on cases found in the books. They liked the requirement of reading a case and responding to the questions posed by the case writer. Several said they had never before been given a requirement to think about a problem and propose a solution to the problem. They liked the freedom to analyze problems and use their knowledge. After the middle of the Fall semester in 1991, I gave them a "take home" writing assignment: "Write a short essay on these questions. (1) What are the major problems facing Romanian managers today? And (2) What are the solutions to the problems facing Romanian managers?"

A variety of responses emerged from this assignment. Some examples of the responses were as follows:

1. An important problem facing a manager nowadays - financial blockage. The payments from the banks are always late and money doesn't circulate from one enterprise to another. This is probably because of the huge factories that are not profitable (too many people are hired and their wages are paid first).

In order to solve this problem of financial blockage an important measure was taken - the convertibility[16] of our <u>leu.</u> It hasn't solved the problem and the blockage still exists, but some action has occurred.

2. I think one of the greatest problems facing managers in our country is the lack of raw materials. Managers have nowhere to obtain them. For instance, there is an important firm in Brasov that produces radiators. It needed copper for this and the only possible way to find it was by establishing agreements with Gypsies by paying them 10,000 *lei* per plate.

I think there are ways to pass over this problem by creating mixed companies with foreign partners. They would come with their capital and advanced technology and work through these problems.

3. During previous years, it was stressed upon enterprises the process of production rather than on marketing or management. These stresses still exist today in the minds of enterprise directors. They can't think in terms of satisfying customer needs or being efficient.

Even if some courses for training are set up, it takes time. A good manager needs especially experience in working in the new situation. Workers also must be trained to accomplish their jobs efficiently.

4. The profound political transformations that took place after December, 1989, ended a period of super-centralized management system and opened the way to pass to a free market economy. One of the greatest problems facing managers and enterprise directors is the adjustment to the characteristics of a free market economy in which an important element is the law of demand and supply.

The Romanian industry has to meet (to cope with) a powerful European and international competition and has to succeed in penetrating different markets. The markets of Eastern Europe and Russia are no longer available in the extent that they were before 1989.

The comments, laboriously written out of class, seemed very perceptive concerning major business problems. The solutions tended to be over-simplistic, but were conceptually correct. If the over-centralization, financial blockage, poor work ethic, supply of raw materials, and incorrect perceptions of managers could be corrected, the country's economy should improve rapidly.

Working with Managers

We were also sent around the country to lecture to practicing managers at their enterprises. These trips were very interesting because they allowed us to speak to managers "on the firing line" and to learn of their concerns. We were told by several middle managers that the factories' general managers were letting the facilities get rundown so that the general manager could buy them for a small amount and then rebuild them as a private enterprises using fewer workers.[17]   We also learned that many industrial facilities did not have enough raw materials for normal operations and not enough energy. Almost all of the factories were unheated in the winter of 1991-92 because there was not enough natural gas available to heat people's homes and the factories also. The Iliescu-Stolohahn government had opted for heating homes rather than factories.

A Questionnaire for Managers

While using a questionnaire with managers which shows how much centralization they practiced in their enterprises, we found that the managers of state enterprises had a higher orientation toward centralization than was found anywhere else in the world. This meant that they were reluctant to make decisions for their enterprise without getting directions from a higher authority.   Conversely, among managers of private companies, we found a very minimal orientation toward centralization: these managers knew that they were independent and needed to make decisions for the survival of their enterprises.   These results were published in the journal *Economic Computation and Economic Cybernetics Studies and Research* in Bucharest in 1995.[18]

Other results from the study of 61 state owned enterprises and 21 private enterprises are shown in the next two tables. The average size among the state owned enterprises, which included factories, transportation companies, restaurants, and hotels (more factories than other type of enterprises) was 2,091 employees. The average size among the private enterprises, which included computer service companies, copier service companies, restaurants, and hotels, was 10.9 employees.

Responses were provided by the enterprise's general manager. I am showing the number one problem and number one remedy stated by the general manager of each enterprise.

Table 1

Major Problems in the Economy

Major Problem	Response State Owned	Response Privately Owned - Enterprise GM
Financial blockage	15	8
Need for investment	11	4
Lack of demand for product	11	1
Inadequate raw materials	9	3
Need to modernize	6	2
Poor management	5	2
Inadequate energy (electricity and/or natural gas)	3	1

Table 2

Remedy for the Major Problem

Remedy	State Owned Enterprises	Private Enterprises
Restructure banking system	13	8
Improve business legislation	8	2
Purchase modern equipment	7	2
Enter into joint venture with a foreign partner	6	2
Improve management skills	6	1
Obtain loans from foreign investors	5	
Privatize enterprise	4	

The most frequent problem voiced by general managers of both state and private enterprises was that of the financial blockage (Table 1). When the enterprise presented a financial instrument (check, draft, letter of credit, etc.) to the banks for hard currency, they would get no payment for at least seven weeks. The holding of hard currency instruments for seven weeks was by order of the president of the national bank, Mugur Isarescu, who had made such a rule for Romanian banks in order that Romania's hard currency reserves would remain high enough to satisfy International Monetary Fund desired levels. However, these long periods in which working funds were kept away from the enterprises made normal business very difficult. This blockage then caused Romanian businesses to withhold payments to their creditors for long periods and it increased the uncertainty of conducting future transactions.

Many of the other major problems and remedies recommended related to the need for capital to run the enterprises (Tables 1 and 2). A few listed the need for improved management and privatization of the enterprise as their major desire. The average number of years until their enterprise was privatized estimated by general managers of state owned enterprises ("How soon will your enterprise be privatized?") was 2.5. Unfortunately, this was an overly optimistic figure, because six years later, most of the enterprises were still in state hands. The General Managers generally favored privatization. Their responses to what the major benefit from privatization would be are shown in Table 3.

Table 3

How Will You Benefit From Privatization?

Benefit	No. of Responses
Better incentives for workers	22
Increased Productivity	18
Increased Level of Business	8
New Equipment	6
Better Financing	4

Romania as a Laboratory

The post-communist culture was a fascinating laboratory for social scientists. Clerks in state owned stores sat behind counters endlessly counting the money they had in their hands. If a customer asked for some assistance, it was a great imposition on the clerk to interrupt the time-consuming activity. In a few instances, we saw state-owned and private stores in close proximity to each other. The prices in the private stores were sometimes higher for the same merchandise, but these private stores were outselling the state-owned stores because of the enthusiasm of the sales people and the service that they were willing to provide. The private stores opened at seven AM and closed at eleven PM, were open twelve to fourteen hours per day and on weekends and were very clean. This was not true for the state owned stores which were not always clean and barely stayed open seven hours per day.

The larger state and private stores had their 'cashier's booths' where payment was made for goods before purchase. Once an item was chosen for purchase from a butcher shop or department store, the purchaser was given a handwritten slip of paper with the price to be paid. The purchaser then had to make payment to the cashier and get another slip of paper, a receipt generated by the cash register, that indicated the amount paid, which would then be taken back to the clerk at the counter where the desired merchandise was exchanged for the receipt. This method put what seemed to be an unnecessary element of control into the transaction and added more people into the sales organization than was needed. It may have come into being as a method to avoid the theft of goods and money by shop employees.

Where there had been almost nothing available in the farmer's markets before the revolution, these open air markets were flourishing in 1991. Not only was fresh produce available during the growing season, but also imported goods were available for sale. Thus we were able to buy powdered milk from the Netherlands, cookies and peanuts from Turkey and Lebanon, chocolate from Germany and Switzerland etc. Even so, Romanians complained incessantly that they did not have enough money to buy what they needed. Their salaries were too low to allow them to buy food and consumer goods in the stores and markets. Yet whenever we went to these stores and markets, there were throngs of people looking at the merchandise and many of them were buying it.

These complaints of having no money were heard from September, 1991, until the present time. The complaints seem to be valid when we see that salaries of professional people average about $100 per month and those of workers are less, while the prices of goods, particularly the imported goods, were very close to the prices paid by westerners. For example, a kilogram of good pork has cost the equivalent of $2.00 and this price was fairly consistent as the leu (the Romanian currency unit; *leu* = lion, plural is *lei*) inflated from 180 *lei* per dollar in 1992 to 3,000 *lei* per dollar in 1996 and 8,600 *lei* per dollar in 1998.

Elections of 1992

Local elections were held in February, 1992, and the Democratic Convention made a strong showing by winning the mayor and city council elections in Bucharest and several other municipalities throughout Romania. After the local elections, the NSF split into two parties; the one still calling itself the National Salvation Front led by former Prime Minister Petre Roman and the other calling itself the Democratic National Salvation Front led by President Ion Iliescu. Roman had called Iliescu the "nostalgic communist,"[19] to try to eliminate the confusion among former NSF adherents as to whom they should support.

Iliescu's position certainly was weakened by the split, but he was able to garner 47 percent of the popular vote in the September, 1992, Presidential election, with Emil Constantinescu of the Democratic Convention in second place with 31 percent. Petre Roman was a distant third place with 10 percent. In the run-off election one month later, Iliescu won with 61 percent of the vote to 39 percent for Constantinescu.[20] The situation was different, however, in the Parliament, with no party approaching a majority. Therefore, a coalition government was formed by the DNSF with former Finance Minister Nicolae Vacaroiu as Prime Minister.[21]

American Embassy staffers considered Vacaroiu a lightweight "interim" Prime Minister, but Vacaroiu surprised them by staying in the job until voted out of office in November, 1996. Vacaroiu was closer to Iliescu than either of the previous Prime Ministers and did not aggressively pursue restructuring and privatization in the economy, although some progress was made because of outside pressures from the IMF and Western Europeans.

Vacaroiu's major program was the introduction of the "Value Added Tax," (VAT) used by many European governments to fund governmental operations. The VAT process taxes goods at every stage of creation for the amount of additional value put in at each stage. Vacaroiu's VAT was at a relatively high level, 18 percent, but it did not solve the government's monetary problems because of the many leaks in the system into the "underground economy." It has been estimated that at least 40 percent of the commerce that was being conducted in the years 1993-1996 was never reported. Much of that commerce was being conducted by managers in state-owned enterprises. The avoidance of taxation and compliance with many of the laws of Parliament was possible because the government's inspectors didn't try to enforce the laws in the state owned enterprises, while they were meticulous in enforcement for private enterprises.

As an example of this practice of "harassment" of private businesses, I once spoke at length with the owner of a newly privatized coffee shop/bakery. He had been running the enterprise for more than a year after refurbishing it completely. His sales were far greater than they had been under the state managers, but his profits were very thin and he could hardly make a living. One of the reasons for this state of affairs was the many inspections and fines he had incurred. When he reopened the coffee shop he had changed its name. He was fined for changing the name of the establishment. He also was fined for putting advertising on the windows where none had appeared under state management. A third fine was levied for putting a fence around his outdoor terrace. Each of these fines was considerable (2 million *lei*, or about $285 at the time they were levied), so he retained an attorney and went to court. He was able to get the fines nullified, but at the cost of his time and his attorney's fees (50,000 *lei*).

As he continued the business, he found himself engulfed by inspectors with overlapping responsibilities. Where we in the U.S. normally designate primary responsibility for an activity to a single level of government, e.g.. Fire inspection, business licensing, and local taxation at the municipal level; education and auto licensing at the state level; federal taxes and interstate commerce at the federal level, the Romanian government had inspectors for many activities at all three levels: municipality, judet (county), and national. Since reopening the coffee shop, it had been inspected by fire inspectors at all three levels, the sanitary police from all three levels, veterinary police from all three levels, economic police from all three levels, League for Protection of Customers from one level, Department of Finance and Pricing from one level, *Guardia Financiare* (tax inspectorate) from National level, City Police from municipality level, and Public Space Administrators at one level. In most of these instances, he sat down and talked with the inspectors, treated them to some cake, coffee, and ice cream, answered their questions and they generally left without causing any problems. Once, when he was sick, a sanitary inspector from the city fined him 200,000 *lei* for a violation in the bakery. Earlier in the same week, a sanitary inspector from the *judet* level had performed an inspection of the premises with him and passed the bakery and the rest of the coffee shop with no problems. On another occasion, a finance inspector fined him 250,000 *lei* because he didn't have an electronic cash register that recorded all transactions (he has one now).

At the same time, his competitors, the state owned coffee shops/bakeries had not sustained any inspections at all. They didn't have electronic cash registers. Their cleanliness and safety conditions were probably inferior to his. His impression is that the "old guard" bureaucrats in the government are hoping to close these upstart private businesses. He feels that they resent his status of being able to keep any profits, if he is ever able to make any.[22]

Privatization of State Owned Enterprises

Over the years since August, 1991, when the Law of Privatization was enacted by the Romanian Parliament, the privatization process has moved in fits and starts, but overall very slowly. Several supplementary pieces of legislation were passed to implement the process in unique businesses such as banking, but even with this legislation, the progress has been slow. Privatization was recognized by outsiders as being extremely important for all former communist countries, with the fundamental belief that private property goes hand in hand with democracy. Since Iliescu and Vacaroiu were not particularly interested in either private property rights or democracy, they did not push privatization unless forced to do so by an outside force such as the International Monetary Fund which had made some amount of privatization a condition for relinquishing funds that had been allocated to help the country rebuild its infrastructure.

Initially, there were about 12,000 enterprises that were in state hands. About half of them were designated for privatization and the day to day control of these enterprises was removed from the government ministries as they were reorganized as "joint stock companies" or "commercial societies" and allowed to have their own board of directors. The other half included the railways, the national airline, the telephone system, the municipal bus and trolley lines, as well as the traditional government monopolies such as the postal service, state radio and television, municipal symphony orchestras and opera companies, and defense industries. Additionally, Romania did not plan to privatize its coal mines, oil wells, and energy distribution enterprises.[23]

As had been described to us in our orientation in September, 1991, the privatization scheme described in Law Number 58 of August, 1991,[24] was to establish five Private Ownership Funds which would own thirty percent of the value of the enterprises in their sphere of interest. Each fund had enterprises in a geographical region, plus some undesirable enterprises. These funds were to be handled similarly to our 'mutual funds,' and as conceived by the consulting firm, Coopers and Lybrandt, would be traded on the stock market once it was established. There was no stock market established when the private ownership fund certificates were issued to citizens in May, 1992. Even with an advertising campaign involving newspapers, radio, and television, there was little recognition among the populace as to what the significance of the certificates actually was. The nominal value of the certificates was 25,000 *lei*, or about $132.00 at the 1992 exchange rate. Some citizens offered them for sale on the street shortly after they were issued for as little as 7,500 *lei*.

Nor was there much movement toward privatization of the companies. The early privatization described in the legislation in 1991 called for 30 large enterprises to be privatized before the end of the year. At the end of the year, no large enterprises had been privatized. In discussions with managers of large enterprises, I learned that there was no set method for evaluating enterprises and the great concern of the private ownership fund directors was that the valuation would be incorrect for an enterprise and it would be sold for less than it was worth.[25]

At the same time, many enterprises were operating at a very low level of productivity due to poor morale of the workforce, inability to obtain raw materials, insufficient electrical power, or low level of demand for the product or service. I visited several research institutes in the Bucharest area in 1992 and heard the same complaint from each of them, "Nobody wants our services anymore. The companies we used to deal with are performing their own research now."

Obviously, during the Ceausescu years, these research institutes had a captive market among the Romanian companies in their areas of expertise. After the revolution, with little demand for the products they could produce, the manufacturing organizations avoided the liability of using an outside research institute to do research for them that probably wouldn't be used. I had a piece of advice for the research managers who complained that "nobody is using us anymore."

"Have you tried to market your services? If not, you need to inform your industry's members what you can do for them."

This idea seemed completely foreign to the research managers. They were still expecting that someone in the Ministry of Industry would direct the manufacturing companies to give all of their research requirements to the "appropriate" research institute. At that time, there were more than one hundred research institutes in the Bucharest area. I revisited two of the research institutes in 1994, Petrodesign and TIAB. The morale was markedly improved by that time and business seemed to be at a satisfactory level. After a bit of discussion with the managers, I found that they had learned how to market their services. Even so, they were looking forward to becoming privatized.

Western Business Enters Romania

Some visitors, both from the west and the far east, came to Romania in the early years after the revolution and left with the impression that rapid progress in business could take place in the newly independent country. They saw much opportunity for foreign investment even though foreign companies would have difficulty in repatriating their profits because the *leu* was not a convertible currency. Companies like Coca Cola and Rank Xerox validated their enthusiasm. Coca Cola had come to Romania in 1992, ten years after Pepsi Cola entered the country. With a huge advertising campaign and a low price strategy, Coca Cola was soon able to outperform Pepsi in Bucharest and the other large cities. Coca Cola established multiple bottling facilities in Romania and may become the soft drink of choice in all parts of the country.

Rank Xerox from the United Kingdom entered Romania in 1990. Its copy machines became very popular with the Romanians who had long been deprived of the right to freely copy anything they wanted. In May, 1992, I interviewed the marketing manager for Rank Xerox's Romanian operations. He said the company's level of business was doubling every six months and the profits on operations were keeping up with the growth. There was competition from Japanese companies, but Rank Xerox held the largest share. The manager said that he couldn't understand why more foreign companies were not making business in Romania. He looked upon the country as a goldmine opportunity.

These rapidly expanding western companies were not concerned that the *leu* was not a convertible currency. They were hiring local people and paying them in *lei*, using some locally procured material when possible which were paid for in *lei*, and in their expansion, they were buying, renting, or building local facilities and paying in *lei* for these expansions. So long as the operations were expanding, they had no concern for repatriating their profits.

Many foreign companies started branches in Romania to fill voids in the Romania economy and took Romanian materials in payment. Companies in Lebanon and Syria sent peanuts, cookies, and chewing gum to Romania and took wood products and potash in return. German and Austrian companies sent electronic goods and took Romanian made clothing in return until their demand for clothing diminished. However, Romania's international trade which had positive balances during the 1980's, often exceeding two billion dollars, became negative in 1990, with a three billion dollar deficit. The country ran one billion dollar deficits in each of the next three years and used up its surplus.[26]

Some other arguments concerning doing business in Romania, pro and con, were summarized in the following statements: "Romania is the third largest market in Eastern Europe and is in desperate need of U.S. products and services. Although the country is still unstable and its laws are changing, many U.S. and Western European companies are entering the market to win long-term market share and avail themselves of Romania's low wages for high-skilled labor."[27] What these authors have said seemed to be true. Romania has an abundance of highly skilled workers and very low wages. However, other problems such as the lack of a convertible currency deterred many investors from putting their money into Romania.

Early Outlook

In the early years, outsiders took on optimistic perceptions of Romania's ability to transition itself into a democratic and a free market economy. At the same time, many Romanians were saying that it would take more than a generation to undo the damage that had been done by the communist regime. We westerners generally passed off these projections as typical Romanian pessimism. Why would it take twenty years? After all, the defeated Axis powers of

World War II had become stable democracies with very strong economies in much less time. We also considered that the Romanians' plea that they needed a 'Marshall Plan' to rebuild their country as unnecessary. The countries of Eastern Europe had not been through a war in fifty years. Besides, assistance efforts had been set up by governments such as the American USIA and USAID programs, British "Know-How" Fund and Western European Tempus Program in addition to private organizations such as the Soros Foundations for an Open Society to help the newly independent states and we thought that they would bring democracy and prosperity in a few years to all of Eastern Europe.

Our initial assessments proved to be incorrect. The transition to democracy and free market in Romania and all of the other Eastern European countries proved to be much more difficult than we had expected on first exposure. While we were giving good advice to the governments of the former communist countries, they were applying the new ideas within a frame of reference that had been created over the last forty-five years. The mentality of the recipients was often not able to accept our 'new' ideas.

Notes

1. George Schopflin, *Politics in Eastern Europe, 1945 - 1992*, (Oxford:Blackwell, 1993), p. 220.
2. Behr, pp. 128-129., and Tismaneanu, p. 17.
3. According to Iliescu, the "Intellectualism" actually was his disagreement with Ceausescu about promoting a North Korean style cult of personality. Iliescu told the National Press Club in Washington on September 27, 1995, that his exile was caused by trying to tell Ceausescu that the Romanian people would not accept a "cult of personality" like that surrounding Kim Il Sung in North Korea.
4. *Scanteia Poporului* (December 23, 1989), pp. 1, 2.
5. Georgescu, p. 289.
6. Marcel Cornis-Pope, *The Unfinished Battles: Romanian Postmodernism Before and After 1989*, (Iasi, Romania: Polirom Co. S.A., 1996), p. 49
7. The subject of our case study, Dana Munteanu, took part in this demonstration.
8. Codrescu, *Hole in the Flag*, p. 189.
9. Cornis-Pope, p. 64.

10. "Romania: Introductory Survey," *The Europa World Yearbook, 1997* Vol. II (London: Europa Publications Limited, 1997), p. 2732.

11. Gallagher, p. 188.

12. "NSF Holds Final Meeting Before Reformation," *BBC Summary of World Broadcasts*, (Bucharest Home Service, Aired on February 3, 1990).

13. My Fulbright award simply stated that I was to "lecture in Business Administration during the 1991/92 academic year." Most of us got involved in activities to assist in the transition in addition to our classroom activities. We were put on programs before citizen groups and even on Romanian national television and asked about our views of the transition process.

14. Vladimir Posner, *Eyewitness: A Personal Account of the Unraveling of the Soviet Union* (New York: Random House, 1992).

15. Also see Roman Frydman, Andrzej Rapaczynski, and John S. Earle, "Romania," *The Privatization Process in Central Europe*, (London: Central European University Press, 1993), pp. 208-262. These authors describe the Romanian process in almost exactly the same terms it was described to me by government officials and enterprise managers in 1991 and 1992.

16. The "convertibility" the student mentioned was internal convertibility which allowed Romanians to trade *lei* for hard currency at a weekly auction. Romanian money was not then and is not now convertible outside of Romania.

17. "When you can't buy food..." *Dividends* (Summer, 1997), p. 7. In this article, as she was looking back, Elena Olariu, former export manager of a Romanian furniture company stated, "It was like a jungle for two years. The managers would try to bankrupt the factories, so they could buy them cheap."

18. J. K. McCollum, A. Coada, and N.K. Mihaita, "Comparison of Management Styles of a Former Socialist Country to Those of Western European Managers," *Economic Computation and Economic Cybernetics Studies and Research*, Vol. XXIX, No. 1-4, 1995, pp. 73-78.

19. Gallagher, p. 122.

20. Ibid., pp. 126-29.

21. Hudelson, p. 140.

22. James K. McCollum, "Astrom United, S.A., Bucharest, Romania," *Case Studies on Economic Transformation: Russia, Kazakhstan and Eastern Europe*, BURK Series, University of Pittsburgh, 1997, pp. 247-257.

23. James K. McCollum, "Romania's First Steps Toward Privatization," in *Struggling with the Communist Legacy*, A Helweg, P. Klein, and B. McRea, eds. New York: Columbia University Press, 1998, p. 180.

24. *Law Digest for Foreign Investors*, (Bucharest: Romanian Development Agency, June, 1992).

25. James K. McCollum, "Romania's Try for the Guinness Book of Records," *Proceedings of the Conferinta Stiintifica Internationala*, Sibiu, Romania, May 16-18, 1996, pp. 78, also Elena Olariu, "If You Don't Have Money to Buy Food," *Dividends* (August, 1997), p. 7.

26. Comisia Nationala Pentru Statistica, *Anuarul Statistic Al Romaniei, 1994*, (Bucuresti: Imprimeriilor Coresi, 1994), p. 597.

27. Carole Flagler and Aurelia Nicoara, "Romania: Land of New Opportunities," *Contract Management* (June, 1994), p. 18.

Chapter 7
More Evidence of the Effects
of Communism

After spending almost half of the last six years in a former communist country, one of my main discoveries was that in spite of the rigid communist ideology that tried to force everyone to feel and act similarly as is found in North Korea, less than half of the population is still affected by the influence of their years under communism and exhibits the coping behaviors described in the case study about Dana Munteanu. This sizeable minority, we will estimate it at 30 per cent, seems to approach things in the same way as before, but the larger portion was not mentally altered by the communist influence. It should be interesting to study how the communist ideology affects some people and not others. What was communism offering to the people?

What was the basic attraction that persists in the minds of the minority that is still affected? In questioning several Romanians about what communism was supposed to provide, we got the following list several times:

1. There was supposed to be complete equality among all of the people: nobody was rich and nobody was poor.
2. Education was free for all students.
3. Everyone received good pensions when they retired.
4. There was free health care for everyone.

We must admit that it was very tempting to want to live in such a society where everyone could have these benefits that society can provide, but the price that was paid was too high and the product that was delivered was seriously flawed. In illustrating these benefits as they were delivered, I am trying to use the ideas of the Romanians as they described their situation. One retired Romanian philosophy professor in Bucharest said:

"Unfortunately, we are not equal, biologically speaking: some of us are stronger mentally, some are stronger physically. This creates differences in what an individual can contribute to society. Some individuals can become scientists while others are more suited to be manual laborers. Partly because of these biological differences, communism was not able to have the same influence on everyone. Some of those with brilliant minds, would refuse to accept the waste of their brainpower to such a system and they refused to be subordinated to a less capable 'superior' who has been promoted because of party loyalty. Thus, communism was on shaky grounds from the beginning because it had the cancer that kills real values of individuals. That's one reason why all of the former communist countries lost the competition in technology - excellent scientists were not given their proper place in society. Communism was the kingdom of fools because it allowed stupid individuals to mock clever people and to make decisions that were not well founded. For these reasons, communism was dead from the beginning."

The Professor continued, "It was not only that the fools were ruling over clever people. Communism destroyed the sense of property, the sense of competition and developed only the sense of fear. The very intelligent scientists and engineers were not allowed to interact with their colleagues from abroad. Many very intelligent individuals were punished for exchanging letters with foreigners. Nobody was allowed to travel abroad except for highly trusted members of the communist party."

So we may ask, what kind of civilized system was this which would not allow normal communications and interactions with the outside world. Communism killed itself through isolation from the outside world. He continued:

"First, we want to make it very clear for every human on earth that we human beings are equal in the face of time, death, and we should be equal in front of the law if the laws are created to defend society. We are fighters in the war to earn our living. We were never meant to be slaves and we are all meant by our creator to find with our own minds the best ways to earn our living within a good legal system that provides a good education for our children and lots of opportunities to develop our abilities, and to build careers according to our abilities. We cannot function as normal, intelligent creatures in a society that tries to plan our lives, our number of children in a family, that plans the number of apples to be harvested from each tree.

"Freedom will forever be the winner. When you keep a bird in a cage it will sing only sad songs. If you let it fly freely in the forest you will hear its the happy chirps. A communist ideologue will say, 'The bird is in great danger. Put it in a cage so it can receive birdseed from its master.' If you give the bird a choice, the bird will always take the risk to fly and enjoy the deepness of the serene blue sky rather than to accept the boring daily portion of food."

So, coming back to my six years in Romania, I'm very happy to say that I have met many open-minded persons, such as Dana Munteanu, the subject of the case study, who were not permanently affected by the draconian rules imposed under the communist era. Somehow, they had been able to escape the brainwashing effects of the system and kept abreast of the newest developments in democratic countries.

Now that I had a chance to judge things better after interviewing hundreds of Romanians, I can say that forty-five years of communism was not a long enough period to change the mentality of the whole people according to one single pattern. Forty-five years is a very long period in a person's lifetime, but not in the entire course of history. In my opinion, the reorientation of the Romanian society toward the normal development took place in the best possible moment. A lot of intelligent and valuable people who had lived between the two world wars and had seen the benefits of a normal free-market economy are still alive. They are in their 80's or 90's, at this time, but they are still ready to describe the "Little Paris," which was the nickname for Bucharest between the two world wars. According to the historical evidence, under the period of monarchy, Romania became a very successful country and the Little Paris was clean, well laid-out, with marvelous architecture and gardens. The Royal Palace was a smaller version of the Louvre, the Chismigiu Gardens in Bucharest were modeled after the Tuillery Gardens, the Bucharest Arch of Triumph is a smaller version of the Paris Arc de Triumph.

One older lady said, "People that have seen the flower battles near Herastrau Gardens could never accept communism as a reality in their country. Wonderful open carriages with elegant people in them were running slowly down the streets and beautiful ladies were throwing large bunches of flowers from one carriage to another during this merry flower festival; a tradition begun before the time of King Carol I. These people who are now in their eighties and nineties have children who are in their sixties and seventies who have memories from their childhood. All of them together during their lives related these memories to their grandchildren, and even the young generation today is aware that Romania, until 1945, was moving toward an open democratic society like that of Italy, France, Portugal, or Spain, the 'Latin Nations' which have evolved into strong democracies in recent years."

More than 50% of the population considers the communist era as a "plague" which affected the country and reversed the development by 100 years. Unfortunately, there is still about 30% of the population which considers that communism was a good system that provided a lot of good features for the population such as good housing, job security, and new facilities such as apartment blocks, roads, subways and free education and health services.

Partly, they are right and we cannot deny that the achievements in these areas occurred, but because of lack of competition the quality of the work became worse every year and the quality of the products and services decreased every year, so that Romania was no longer able to export any products that were readily accepted in foreign markets except foodstuffs. Consequently, in the latter years of the Ceausescu regime, the population was no longer able to buy the usual food for themselves because such a large percent of it was being exported. So, in the face of the marvelous resources possessed by Romania: agriculture, tourism, chemical industry, minerals, etc, due to bad management imposed by the communist system, Romania became an economic failure. Romania was still providing the same bountiful produce from its fertile soil for huge crops, wide orchards and vineyards, plus food for livestock such as cattle, sheep, pigs and poultry. All that was needed was better organization and management for production which is now evolving under free market conditions.

Right after the December, 1989 revolution, conditions changed rapidly. The first beneficiaries were the peasants. They no longer had to fear that their villages would be destroyed and their land taken away; No longer would communist administrators count their livestock and claim half of it for the state. The peasants began immediately to buy more cattle and sheep because they no longer had to fear that the state would take away their calves, lambs, wool, milk and cheese. Romanian peasants are very hard working people.

They began to repair their village houses because they no longer had to fear that they would lose their houses and be forced to move into bloc apartments. They cultivated food products around their houses to provide food for animals. For example, in one village of 500 families near Targoviste, there were only 50 cows in the entire village in 1989. Now, there are 500 cows, a ten-fold increase.

The Iliescu government did not tax the farmers in the early years and allowed them to reclaim up to ten hectares of land to be held privately. This was a mixed blessing, because they did not have their own tools which had previously been taken by the collective forms, but even so, the farmers launched into private production with gusto which brought increases in output almost immediately. The farmer's markets all over the country which had been barren were quickly inundated with all kinds of high quality food: meat, cheese, milk, and vegetables.

However, Romania is no longer a predominantly agricultural society. More than 60% of the work force is nonagricultural. Many of these workers are employed by the industrial dinosaurs built by the Ceausescu regime which are producing low quality goods that are not in demand by consumers. What is the government supposed to do about those dinosaurs? This is one of the most difficult problems to be solved by the new government. The government under President Emil Constantinescu, elected in November, 1996, wants to either close these non-productive energy consumers, or privatize them. In either situation, many workers will lose their jobs. Some laws have been promulgated by the parliament under Prime Minister Victor Ciorbia to encourage young people who still have relatives in the country to become farmers. They can obtain grants of land of up to 10.5 hectares at no cost to themselves if they will return to their villages work the land.[1]

Interim Assessment

Let's now go back to the beginning of the story to show why conditions are so complicated today. What happened during the forty-five years of communism?

(1)   OK, the educational system was free - everyone could go to elementary, secondary, and institutions of higher education, but when the graduates went forth to their new job positions, the graduates found that they were not allowed to think for themselves and apply

their knowledge, because promotions were based on loyalty to the communist party and its dogmatic hierarchy rather than by meritorious service. The quality of products declined continuously because engineers and scientists were not stimulated to perform well. Professional workers went forth to their jobs like robots because they had no professional motivation. Even more disheartening was the Ceausescu decision in 1974 that all workers must have a high school education. Teachers and administrators were forced to promote everyone without any competition.

Once students learned that they would advance from class to class without any possibility of failure, they lost all interest in studying. From that time onward, many high school graduates could barely read and write, but still received diplomas. You might say that the educational system was effectively destroyed. Many graduates didn't learn anything about culture, art, sciences, mathematics, or any of the normal high school disciplines. We can find many "electricians" who are practicing this craft today, but know little about electricity, also plumbers, carpenters, mechanics, etc., who do not know the skills they were supposed to have learned in high school. Teachers and administrators lost their prestige because they had no possibility to discipline students who refused to complete homework assignments. Everyone knows that children are by nature lazy and prefer to play with various means of entertainment. Children like to watch TV, play football, and listen to music. As Pink Floyd told us about twenty years ago, "We don't need no education; teachers leave the kids alone." This philosophy became reality for many students under the Ceausescu regime. Normally, a well organized society is based on a very well organized educational system.

Education starts from kindergarten where the curriculum is mainly concentrated upon values of good citizenry. A child should gradually find out that life is a struggle and in order to have a chance to be a "winner" he or she needs a lot of knowledge about life skills, needs to identify his or her skills and talents to build a successful career upon. The classes and games prepare them for the competition for later educational pursuits. When a child matriculates from a kindergarten, the germ of ambition to become the best in the group, or the best they can be, should have already been implanted. Meanwhile, children have to be impressed with the reality that working at educational activities, that fair play, and justice bring about the desired rewards. If they don't obtain this orientation, they will have no confidence that hard work and honest dealings bring success.[2]

Once children are convinced that they should do the right things, they should get the right rewards such as good grades and recognition. This will build self confidence and a sense of justice in a child's mind. The children will then be mentally prepared for the progression of more difficult subjects which will lead to later success in life. Meanwhile, as we said, no matter how self confident they are, many students tend to be lazy. It should be a role of teachers to motivate them to excel. In the *gymnasia* (middle schools) and high schools, the teachers should be able to hold back unmotivated students to get them to perform well, and the teachers should continue to stress that good citizenship is the key to success to living a decent and successful life.

Preparation for a productive life normally entails being well trained for a certain job so that the student can find a good working place with a good salary which will provide the opportunity for marriage and children with good support and a successful family which has good food on the table, comfortable housing, means for vacations. Such a family becomes a proper building block of the society.[3]

When the teachers of Romania lost control of being able to discipline their students after 1974, the students realized that no what did or did not do, they would graduate and the whole system of promoting civic values fell. The only possibility to educate good specialists in various fields was saved for the universities and polytechnic institutes because there, the student's future jobs were dependent upon the grades obtained. Those students who obtained good grades had a chance to get a job in the cities and towns: others were relegated to villages and countryside areas.

The system worked like this: students from all over the country were given an examination for university admission in the cities which had universities. The admission exam was the only competition that rewarded talented students based on merit and this screening only applied to one-half of the places for each new class. Half of the places were reserved for the children of party leaders. Many of those party favorites were not capable of performing university level studies, but again the edict, "Don't give failing grades to party leaders children," prevented them from failing. Romania graduated many scientists and engineers who knew no more than their shoemaker president.   Once they were admitted to the university, they knew that their jobs awaited with no struggle.   But, the jobs were spread all over the country and the assignment of jobs was accomplished based on grades.   If a student was from Bucharest and received low grades, the government would provide a job somewhere in the countryside, while those from the countryside with good grades got good jobs in Bucharest.   The initial job was established under a contract for three years and the graduates had to spend those three years where they were assigned.   This system resulted in sending many graduates away from their homes and families brought about much unhappiness.

Students who had gotten married during their university days often were separated: the husband assigned to Craiova, the wife to Tulcea, or the wife to Oradea and the husband to Iasi, or the husband stayed in Bucharest while the wife was sent to Petrosani, as we saw in our case study.   Romania normally has close knit family relations and little geographic mobility among job holders, therefore this action caused a lot of sorrow and many family problems. This trauma also resulted in lack of motivation in the graduates who found themselves as strangers among strangers.

(2) Of those approximately thirty percent of the population who regret the demise of the communist system are those who were happy to obtain a job without competition.   These people were not well prepared to hold jobs, but were assured that they would have them under the communist system.   Thus that part of the population is not mentally prepared for the normal struggle of earning a living because they have no confidence in their own skills and abilities and cannot compete in the jobs market when the free market economy is fully implemented.

On the other side, the children from the country areas had no opportunities to earn a living from their little farms so they were forced to become workers in the huge plants built during the communist era.   They came to the big cities and most became accustomed to city life and are not willing to go back to the land after they were given land ownership in the post revolution era.   They see the work in the rural areas as too arduous.   Unfortunately, the training system for these displaced farmers was not good and they often were not able to perform the work they were assigned.   In most factories, the work force included at least twice as many workers as would be found in factories in free market countries. The hallmark of success for managers was that of having a large work force, not efficiency within the workforce.

The lack of training of the workers prevented efficiency. Being in this position, the workers were aware that they were not well specialized to find jobs in other factories and they did not want to go back to the land. This situation will create a larger and larger pool of unemployed workers who are unskilled for city work and unwilling to perform country work.

(3) But, before destroying the educational system which probably was not a communist intent, the communist system was very open in its drive to destroy the sense of private property. All of the farmers lost their lands and their tools because they were forced to give all of their assets to the CAP (*Cooperativa Agricola de Productia*). The leaders said, "This is communism. We will have all of the land, all of the tools, and all of the livestock held in common from now on." However, not being the owners of the land any longer, the farmers didn't feel responsible anymore, so instead of having better production, because of the lack of interest in their work, the production decreased. Beyond that, some of the farmer were tempted to steal, because they said, "No one will notice if we steal from the state, the state is big and won't miss what we take." They started to send their children to schools to become workers in the big factories because the work in the *Cooperativa Agricola Productie* (CAPs) was hard and worthless. Even if they were no longer true peasants anymore, the workers in the CAPs received no salaries, only a small portion of the produce from their cooperatives and at the end of their life's work, they received a very small pension. In their own courtyards, they were still allowed to own one or two cows, but they were obligated to give half of the milk produced and all of the calves to the CAP.

The same occurred in the big factories. The leaders said that the factories belonged to everybody and thus nobody owned anything. Since the sense of private property was destroyed most of the population lost all motivation to produce. The worker population started to think and act like robots. If they were peasants, they knew that they would have to work for the rest of their lives for pensions of 90 lei per month (approximately $13.00 at the 1989 conversion rate). Those who became workers in the factories knew that they would get the same small salaries no matter what was the quality of their work. There was a saying during the Ceausescu years, "*Timpul trece, leafa merge, Noi cu drag muncim*" ("Time passes, the salary comes, we "happily" go on working.") Or there was another saying,

Cine-I harnic, si munceste	The one who works hard
Are tot ce vrea	has all that he needs
Cine-I lenes, si chuileste	The one who is lazy
Are mai ceva.	Has more than he needs.
Cine-I harnic, si munceste	The one who works hard
Ori e prost, ori ne gandeste.	Is either stupid or doesn't think at all.

Thus the sense of responsibility was very poor and the work ethic was poor.

For all of the above reasons, communism killed itself. The ultimate product of the society diminished in quality every year.

Several philosophic Romanians have waxed eloquently to me during informal meetings with ideas along these lines: "What actually is a human being? One aspect is that it is a creature who is able to think. Think of what? Of the values of his or her life. Human nature is mainly characterized by certain senses: 1) sense of freedom, 2) sense of justice, 3) sense of property, 4) sense of value, 5) sense of beauty, 6) sense of dignity, 7) sense of morality, and others.

1. Sense of freedom. A normal human wants to know as much as possible about the surrounding environment. He or she is sociable and has a strong sense of communication. Humans want to socialize, to have friends, to travel, to get access to all kinds of useful information. But, the communist leaders decided they wouldn't allow people to travel abroad, to have foreigners as friends, to exchange letters or information. They would have liked to destroy all of the books that can bring illumination to people's minds and souls. They wouldn't accept television except for two hours a day on a single channel. They wouldn't buy or bring foreign movies to Romania in the last ten years. They even decided in the last five years that it was too expensive to have a children's channel on TV. So what was communism trying to do? To kill the normal sense of freedom in human nature. Fortunately, it proved to be impossible. No matter how hard they tried to build walls and barriers around the country, outside information was still able to penetrate and to circulate. The marvelous literature of Dickens *(Great Expectations, Oliver Twist)*,

Sallinger *(Catcher in the Rye)*, Shakespeare, Faulkner, Dumas, *(The Three Musketeers, The Count of Monte Cristo)*, and Mark Twain *(Tom Sawyer, Huckleberry Finn, A Connecticutt Yankee in King Arthur's Court)* was still available. Besides the marvelous books that helped to keep the hopes of the Romanian people alive, some radio broadcasts in the Romanian language from The Voice of America and Radio Free Europe told the Romanian people the truth of what was going on with the communist system. Thirty percent of the population knew the truth of communism's failures from listening to these broadcasts (which the Romanian *Securitate* tried unsuccessfully to block). This thirty percent was expecting the momentary demise of the communist economic system. Thus communism was totally oriented against the fundamental human and "unalienable rights... life, liberty and the pursuit of happiness." (Thomas Jefferson)

2. Sense of Justice. In the course of history, human societies have developed a strong sense of justice. A normal human being can immediately determine what is inherently right from what is wrong. It was not right to promote someone just because he was a party leader's friend. It was not just to give the bonus to the chief engineer for an innovation instead of giving to the engineer who devised it. It was not just to use the industrial workers, students and soldiers to harvest the crops on the CAP lands while CAP workers stood on the sidelines and ridiculed them. It was not just to use the industrial workers during their normal working time to "wet" the agricultural land with pails because the irrigation system was not working and then lie about production figures. So communism was able to kill the sense of justice. Everyone was trying to be smart to obtain benefits through illegal means so that someone who was a tractor driver would use the tractor for personal purposes after the workday and those who were working on a bridge or block of flats would steal cement and bricks for their own purposes. Workers at the slaughter houses have been caught sending stolen meat packed in plastic bags down the Dimbovita river (the river that flows through Bucharest). So, the communist system not only killed the sense of justice, but also the sense of honesty and morality.

3. Sense of Property. The greatest injustice that was committed was the expropriation of privately owned homes, lands, factories, animals, tools, and objects of art. At the beginning of the communist era, the cities were much smaller than they are today and the biggest losers were the peasants. There were not so many owners of homes

and factories at that time, although there have been 800,000 claims to recover expropriated homes since 1991. (Less than one third have been recovered in mid-1997) The Lion's share of the population was among the peasants, and they lost everything.

The retired Bucharest philosophy professor said, "All human beings have a deep sense of property ownership. There are also members of the animal kingdom which defend their "territory" on which they live and hunt. Thus we cannot blame a human being for feeling that he is lost without his property. Once a human owns property, he will strongly feel responsible for it and will fight for it and work to improve and enlarge it because it brings a purpose in his life. One who has no property has nothing to leave to his heirs. But communism wanted above all to kill the sense of private property. Thus, a family was allowed to have only one house on a small piece of land if they were living in the countryside and everything was kept under strong control so that nobody was allowed to become financially dangerous to the system. A well managed property brings money to the owner. Even so, peasants were relatively happy with their little houses and few animals. However, the people in the cities were relegated to ghettos called "blocs of flats" with extremely small rooms and very small kitchens. The largest part of the city dwellers were living in this kind of ghetto - a dull life with no joy, no future, hearing the neighbor using the toilet in the next flat through the thin walls. At last everything was shared in common. Then began the rationing in 1975, when families were restricted to shopping in a designated *alimentara* (grocery store) where they were required to show their identity cards and sign for the monthly allocated amounts: 2 kilos of cooking oil, 2 kilos of sugar, and 2 kilos of flour. Meat, cheese, butter and many other food items were practically nonexistent. At least the leaders were not clever enough to tell the workers, "Look, buddy, this 'lathe' is yours to do with it what you want." But the lathe had no owner and received no maintenance and lubrication. "Why should I care about this lathe. It is not mine. Tomorrow, my supervisor can send me to another machine. Let the real owners take care of it."

"So, the sense of property was destroyed. So the sense of responsibility died with it. So the good quality of the products died with it. So the market for the products died with it. So communism should be dead forever!" exclaimed the professor.

4.   Sense of values.   In a society where the promotion of

individuals is based on other criteria than real value, it is normal that in the course of time, people became confused about real values. It was not worthwhile anymore to try make achievements honestly and those who were successful through dishonest means were amply rewarded. Those who took advantage of their positions to extort bribes from the population to get them to do what was nominally their assigned jobs were well accepted and covered by the communist system. This, of course, implied a lot of corruption. The institution of *bacsis* (bribe or tip) became a well established art under the communist system. In a speech to the Parliament in December, 1990, The National Peasant Party presidential candidate, Ion Ratiu declared, "Our country used to be a happy country. Communism destroyed it. Communism destroyed the person and destroyed his internal integrity, his self respect, honesty, correctness-"[4]

If a writer wanted to get any works published and attain any recognition, he had to praise the communist system throughout the article or book and quote from the ghost written books of the most wonderful "Son of the People," President Ceausescu. A writer was only considered to be a valuable one if he picked all of his subjects from the "marvelous" achievements of the communist era. The truly valuable writers and philosophers no longer were published. Musical composers also had to uses lyrics that praised the communist system. A large number of false writers and poets emerged who promoted the "cult of personality" for the Ceausescu couple. Valuable actors were forced to recite poems dedicated to Nicolae and Elena Ceausescu on TV. This created a ridiculous situation; everyone felt sick of hearing, day and night, that Nicolae Ceausescu was the most beloved "son of the people." Everybody was disappointed at this exaggeration of the cult of personality, so they made fun of it and mocked it.

Here is one of the jokes of that time: "Ceausescu and his wife took a vacation in one of his summer palaces. Ceausescu went onto the terrace to admire the beautiful landscape and the morning sun. He was move to say, '*Buna dimineata, soare* (Good morning, sun.)' Then he heard a voice which said, 'Good morning, Mr. President.' He went back to his wife, and said, 'Look, Elena, even the sun is greeting me!' The next morning, he told her, 'Come with me and you'll see.' When she joined him, he shouted loudly, 'Good morning, *soare* (sun.)' and a voice answered, 'Good morning Mr. President. But I'm Colonel Vasile, Colonel Soare was on duty yesterday.'" In spite of the fact that he knew that everyone was mocking him, he went on with the story of the cult of personality until the end.

Together with the death of the senses we described above, there was also a strong depreciation of the senses of morality, dignity, and beauty. Instead of trying to improve their educations, the young, being mostly confused, were not attracted to good literature and music and instead became vulgar and bawdy. In the early 1980s. Good quality folk music was replaced by gypsy music containing a lot of obscenities in the lyrics. Even the usual wedding music was replaced by gypsy and Turkish music.

The reaction against the marvelous Romanian folk music was caused by Ceausescu's propaganda officers forcing the folk singers to exchange the old lyrics with new, stupid ones like, *"Badita mi-e tare dor, Sa te vad iar pe tractor."* (My dear, I'm longing to see you again on the tractor). For such reasons, the young began to abandon the adulterated folk music.

All societies which might attempt to build a utopian system should realize that they are wasting time and resources because a society of robots is contrary to nature. Each human being is unique. If we simply take the example of fingerprints, we know that no two people out of the six billion people on the earth have the same fingerprints or DNA. How can there be any chance that all people can have the same personality. Attempts to create such automatons will result in a reaction which produces the opposite effect of that desired. The only result is that the people will starve, e.g. North Korea in 1997.

I was and still am surprised that nobody bothered to explain and to repeat the simple explanation that the communist system is dead forever. No famous writer from abroad or from Romania has explained that people need a simple explanation that communism is a worthless utopia. That's why I feel that I am responsible to make a revision of   arguments that communism is a false dream- it's something that gives false hopes but results in failed realities.

If we go back in time to see how everything started, we must admit that there appeared to be many injustices in the capitalist era. The rich were tempted to keep all of the benefits for themselves and would not share these benefits with workers, but as we learned from Adam Smith in 1776 and Milton Friedman in the present time, those who act in their own self interest serve society because they produce exactly what the society needs. Besides that, they create the jobs society needs.

The first mistake under communism in Romania occurred when the workers decided they could rule the society rather than of gradually obtaining these rights in a well organized civic society. Workers decided that they could occupy the top governing and managing positions without educating themselves to these important tasks. The workers decided that intellectuals are dangerous because they can analyze situations and discover the mistakes being made by worker decision makers. They went so far that they would not accept as students in the universities any candidates except children of workers and peasants. This restriction continued during the 1950's and into the 1960's in Romania. Even after that, to get a managerial position required a "good" file, i.e., one that showed that your parents had been workers or peasants.

Thus the struggle against intellectuals went on and on. Once the workers became the rulers of society in 1946, they immediately made the decision to destroy private property. The workers hadn't foreseen that if there were no longer any owners (owners of land, property, tools, etc.) that the former owners would feel dispossessed and would not be motivated to serve these new masters. Everyone, former intellectuals, former workers former peasants, experienced alienation in the "new" society. Nobody knew exactly how they fit in it.

How could a former train worker (Gheorghiu-Dej) or a former shoemaker (Ceausescu) rule over intellectuals and scientists? Only through terror which destroyed all opposition. Nobody could oppose any of their decisions and not be punished.

We can always aim for a better society, a society that provides protection for all of its members. A society that is promoting the real values and has a deep sense of justice in all fields. What we are speaking about is a real democracy. A democracy means that we are all equal, yet of each of us is unique. We are all equal under the law. A beggar or a president should receive the same punishment for breaking a particular law. Right now, there are many well organized democratic societies: e.g., Germany, France, England, Canada, the USA. Have you ever heard of a West German trying to emigrate to a communist country? Even if the German worker is not as rich as his factory owner, he is satisfied with the conditions his society is providing for him. The same story is true of American workers. There are lots of millionaires in the USA and rather than trying to destroy them, we admire them. That is because the opportunity exists for anyone to become a millionaire and the US government provides the environment to assist the ambitious people.

All democratic societies provide the best conditions for managers, engineers, scientists, inventors, musicians, writers and artists who have marketable talents, products, inventions, literature and fine arts. A democratic society is the one which allows a citizen to develop his/her talents and abilities. If someone has talents and abilities, no one will stop him or her from developing it. On the contrary, they will be encouraged to use these talents for the benefit of society while the individual with the talent reaps great benefits also. Then if we are speak about people without significant talents, they can also be happy with their jobs, because according to democratic rules, they can move up in status. According to the democratic rules, they are always able to take jobs with better salaries by job changes or to improve their existing salaries through negotiating or strikes. What everybody needs is democracy and freedom, not communism and isolation: Freedom to get into the Internet and learn what is happening all over the world, freedom to exchange scientific information to everyone in the world, freedom to travel and have friends all over the world.

Because communism was not good for individuals, but was a dictatorship, and we still have dictatorships and we still have oppressed people in the world, we need to tell everyone the truth and teach them how to fight for their rights. We are all citizens of this marvelous planet called earth. We should all concentrate our efforts to keep the planet in good health so that we can enjoy our short lives in peace and harmony.

A Businessman's View of Communism

One young (early 40's) Romanian businessman who had worked several years as an engineer in a factory before the revolution gave these beliefs about communism and the communist system. He was reflecting both on what communism did before the revolution and what the former communists who still have political power are doing now.

"Communism appeared as an ideology in a time when mankind was changing in many ways: economically, socially, and politically. In this period, various theories for organization of society, organization for the economy, and organization for the state came forth.

"One theory that gained a large audience for the working class was communism. What was it that communism wanted to do for society?

1) Property should be held in common so that the different social classes would disappear. There would be no more rich and poor people. What happened in fact? Property was held in common, but it was not well organized and used. This resulted in total lack of efficiency in all fields of the society. It was true that social classes disappeared, but instead of everyone being able to earn a decent life, there was a general poverty and more than that, new social classes appeared: *nomenclatura, securitatia,* and the large mass of ordinary people. People's interest toward work decreased because everybody thought they were working enough for the humble monthly salary they received, a salary that wasn't large enough to cover their primary needs.

2) Property held in common needed centralized planning because the state was responsible for all activities. The state turned out to be a very poor administrator and proved to be not able to identify the demands of the market. The economy was based on the principle that all people should have a place to work, no matter what the quality of their products would be. This was to avoid unemployment and to demonstrate communism is better than capitalism which always has large amounts of unemployment. The goods produced were sold only in the markets where the product was the only one available. At that time, COMECON, the communist economic organization for the communist block, was providing a semi-international market for the products of all the communist countries and in this organization all countries were accepted with its products for the sake of the communist ideology. Romanian products were also being sold in Arabic and African countries where they were more inexpensive and affordable than products from western countries. Good products produced in free market economies were forbidden from the markets of communist countries. Some of the poor quality communist made products were not accepted anywhere and stocks of these unwanted products brought about a financial blockage.

3) In a planned, centralized economy, there was no competition. Lack of competition resulted in very bad quality for all products and it resulted in a very poor organization of the labor force with much

inefficiency. These factors caused low productivity.

4) Lack of efficiency caused the destruction of the economic capacity of the entire system. The ultimate result was a very low standard of living for the people. There was, at the same time, an interdiction of information about what was available in free market countries. Romania became like a sick, paralyzed person. In order to keep the *nomenclatura*, a ferocious dictatorship emerged which endangered the citizens even more than before. The mere hearing of information other than that propagated by the communist dictator was a great infraction of the law and people who dared to taste even a little bit of freedom: sending and receiving letters and packages from friends abroad, listening to the Radio Free Europe and Voice of America and telling others about what was being said from these sources, were convicted and sent to prison. A system of terror was created to keep the populace in line. Men were terrorized by other men. From this point of view, communism is the most ferocious system ever devised, destroying people's self will. The dictator destroyed the people's right to communicate freely, the right to live without fear. Communism produced the largest number of victims trying to save its dead principles. The people accepted the fate of having to stand in long lines at the food shops or long lines at the gasoline stations and had no other desires in life than to fulfill these basic needs. They accepted the requirements to form huge demonstrations of support for the "cult of personality" because they had no means to fight against it. People became accustomed to considering that they were receiving the means of sustaining life as a gift from the state rather than as a result of their own work. The continuous degradation of the living standard finally brought about the changes in Eastern Europe and the people of these countries are now trying to gradually move toward normal conditions, but the difficulties are very large. The people's mentality has been altered during the oppression they endured for almost fifty years - they have been accustomed to receive and accept all guidance in life from the government. They find now it to be extremely difficult for them to think and judge what is good and what is bad and how to make up their minds on how to earn their living.

"People expected to receive a house to live in from the enterprise where they work. College students expected to obtain a good job as soon as they graduated and receive a high salary that will cover all of their needs, but they were not willing to offer a good quality of work in return. The workers came to work as robots - they didn't care what work was done, how work was done, what results came from their efforts. These aspects didn't concern the worker - all he wanted was to receive a good salary at the end of the month.

"The chief executives of the factories are former communist party activists and they consider that this is the moment to become owners of state assets without thinking that they have no means to save the enterprises. They have no capitalization. So managers are blocking privatization now because they don't want to lose their positions with privileges included. More than that, the former members of the securitate, the *tortionari* (most rabid members) have taken advantage of the lack of information and knowledge of the population regarding the free market economy system and they believe that they have good opportunities to control everything by introducing the methods of a very primitive form of capitalization which has very small group of rich while the larger part of the population is poor forever. They are not interested in providing a modern standard of living for the population and a modern economy. They do not need a large, strong middle class of honest entrepreneurs. They are only interested in getting more and more assets through illegal means with a total disregard for laws. They are still manipulating the population using various diversions such as selling apartments that belonged to the state to high government officials for much less than the real value to gain influence with these officials and to be able to blackmail them at any moment.

"The average citizen is not able yet to fight for democracy knowing exactly what this means. The average citizen doesn't know that the people in power are supposed to inform the population about the results of the administration of the country.

"The average citizen does not know yet that property rights must be safeguarded, that the right to information must be respected. The average citizen is still manipulated by various unscrupulous interests. The conclusion is that communism was able to mentally transform the people, but communism could not provide an acceptable standard of living because if this had been possible, all of mankind would have been gradually buried in communism and the simple man turned into an animal who was not supposed to think but only to work and eat a little bit. We are extremely lucky that communism was not successful."

Notes

1.   *Romania Libera*, June 27, 1997, p. 1.
2.   Laurence Kohlberg, "Stage and Sequence: The Cognitive-Developmental Approach to Socialization," in *Handbook of Socialization Theory and Research*, D.A. Goslin, ed. (Chicago: Rand McNally, 1969), pp. 347-380.
3.   John Kenneth Galbraith, *The Good Society*, New York: Houghton Mifflin Company, 1995, pp. 133-35.
4.   *Rompress*, December 21, 1990.

Chapter 8
Former Communist Countries Now and in the Future

The problems of transitioning all of the newly independent states into functioning free market democracies is turning out to be much more difficult than many of us predicted in the early years after the fall of the Berlin Wall. In 1996, Marcel Cornis-Pope told us in his book, *The Unfinished Battles*, "The consensus among analysts is that East Europe's transition to post communism has barely started and that it has not yet involved a major post-totalitarian reconstruction."[1] Vladimir Tismaneau also has stated concerning the demise of communist regimes that the "slow pace of the national purification needs to confront the resilient communist customs - all the habits, mentalities, attitudes, symbols, and values that have permeated social life for decades."[2]

In a book written in 1991, *How We Survived Communism and Even Laughed,* Croatian writer Slavenka Drakulic admitted, "The title of my book feels wrong,... We have not yet survived communism, and there is nothing to laugh about."[3] How prophetic the statement was! The horrors of the war in Yugoslavia were to engulf the country and lead to hundreds of thousands of deaths and unspeakable atrocities by Serbs, Croats, and Bosnians. In an epilogue to the same book written in November, 1992, she stated, 'I still don't understand what this war is even now...how much this war is the legacy of communism and the repression of national and religious feeling, the lack of civil society, its values and institutions.'[4]

While the mechanisms for democracy and free market have been established, they are not yet functioning well. In a later book, Croatian writer Slavenka Drakulic tells us that East Europeans have been in sort of a "purgatory" since 1989. They have shaken themselves loose from the forces of repression and slavery but have yet to make it to an acceptable accommodation with democracy. Having elections where there is more than one name on the ballot for each position is not necessarily the same as democracy and once you penetrate the facade of democratic activity, you still discover a communist-like mentality.[5]

The continued presence of the "political police" in Romania long after the fall of communism prompted Andrei Codrescu to say in one of his National Public Radio "All Things Considered" monologues, "Only in a few countries of the former Red Empire are the secret police still employed. In Romania they still run things, though its more and more on a free lance basis."[6]

As we have previously stated, it has been an article of faith among political reformers that the evolution of democracy and free market economics go hand in hand. Without the one, the other probably will not work. The mechanism for both can be enacted in legislation, but until the mentality of a majority of the citizens has changed, neither aspect is firmly established. Can we say that free market economics are truly present in the newly independent states?

Economic Transition

In September, 1990, my wife, Barbara, and I, were revisiting Germany for the first time since the mid-1960s. We encountered a contingent of young (30 to 40 year old) Germans from the former East Germany one evening in the Hofbrauhaus in Munich. These young Germans were making their first "legal" visit to what had been, as the Bundesrepublic of Germany forbidden to them before 1989. In our conversations with them, we became aware that the new "Greater Germany" was divided into four frames of mind about the transition. We knew that older, former West Germans were very happy to have the country reunited because they had friends and relatives they could see again. The younger West Germans, however, were not so enthusiastic, because they knew that the burden for paying for the reunification would fall on their shoulders. Conversely, the young East Germans were very happy that the Berlin Wall had fallen because they would then be allowed to live in an economic system that rewarded initiative and hard work.

But, we learned that the older East Germans were upset because the change had occurred. They had lived more than forty years under communism and their futures had been assured - a pension, free health care, and a certain status for being a good comrade now would be lost and their futures would be uncertain. For these older east Germans, they would prefer to return to the command economy of communism because of the greater certainty in their lives. We have heard Romanians actually say, "We wish Ceausescu was still in power." Their new freedoms and market opportunities don't seem to be as important to them as a well-ordered (though repressed) existence, or else they are not remembering the bad old days of communism very well.

In 1993, Marianne Gentle-Marsh and I undertook an extensive study of the economic transformations in Central and Eastern Europe. Our research, using the Lexis and Nexis search engine, focused on the positive changes that were being made in eight of the newly independent states, but we didn't find a great amount of positive indicators in these eight economies. In our conclusions to the study, we said, "Although many Eastern European and former Soviet countries had progressed down the path of economic reform leading to market-based economies by early 1993, most were still relatively unstable. Productivity is down; inflation and unemployment are up in all of the former socialist countries."[7] (See Table 4, reproduced from pp. 975 & 976 of the article).

As can be seen in these more recent figures (Table 5), the economies of the three nations accepted for entry into NATO, Czech Republic, Hungary, and Poland are improving at a faster rate than those of the other nations, Bulgaria, Romania, Russia, and Ukraine. The GDP per capita of the best performers is far less than is found in western countries and the average monthly wages are minuscule compared to those in developed countries.

Political Transformations

Some of the more progressive of the newly independent states, Poland and Hungary, unseated their democratic governments two

TABLE 4
COUNTRY COMPARISONS

	ALBANIA	BULGARIA	CZECHOSLOV.	HUNGARY	POLAND	ROMANIA	RUSSIA	UKRAINE
Size (sq. miles)	10,000	42,000	49,381	35,919	120,825	91,699	4,280,000	235,000
Population	3,200,000	9,000,000	15,600,000	10,600,000	38,000,000	23,000,000	147,300,000	51,400,000
State ownership (before privatization)		96%	97%	100%	82%	90%	100%	100%
Companies to be privatized			2,000 large 3,000 small	2,500	5,000	6,280		
Employee ownership plan				yes	yes	yes	yes	yes
Voucher system			yes	no	yes	yes	yes	yes
Price liberalization (yr.)	95% (92)	(91)	85% (91)	90% (91)	95% (92)	95% (92)	(92)	
Privatization law	1991	1992	1990	1989	1993	1991	1992	1992
Amt. privatized (no. of enterprises end of '92)		100,000 small	500 lg. & med.	330 lg. & med.	80,000 small	2 large	13,739	
New enterprises (92)				500,000	1,200,000	300,000		
Unemployment	50%		2.5% Czech R. 10.4% Slov.	12%	13.2%	10%	10%	
Convertible currency	no	no	no	(1994)	yes (1991)	no	no	no
Industrial output (yr.)	-50% (91)	-20% (90)	-20% (91)	-6.5% (91)	-25% (90) -15% (91)	-20% (90) -22% (91)	-20% (92)	-20% (92)
Inflation (yr.)	250% (91)		50% (91)	34% (91) 27% (92)	40% (92)	323% (91)	350% (92)	225% (92)
Heritage Foundation Grade (9/92)	I	B-	B	B+	B	C		

TABLE 5
COUNTRY COMPARISON, 1997

	BULGARIA	CZECH REP	HUNGARY	POLAND	ROMANIA	RUSSIA	UKRAINE
GDP 1991	$8.1 billion	$32.3 billion	$33.4 billion	$76 billion	$28.9 billion	$801 billion	
GDP 1997	$10.3 billion	$52.1 billion	$45 billion	$134 billion	$34.6 billion	$473.6 billion	$48.7 billion (1996)
Change in GDP	+27%	+61%	+35%	+76%	+20%	-41%	
GDP/cap 1997	$3,758	$11,574	$7,290	$6,407	$4,364	$4,361	$2,206
Monthly avg. wage	$75.50 (1996)	$334.50 (1997)	$310 (1997)	$352.50 (1997)	$121.80 (1997)	$181.90 (1997)	$86.00 (1996)
Inflation 1997	1082.2%	8.5%	18.3%	14.9%	154.7%	14.6%	15.9%
Unemployment 1997	13.7%	5.2%	10.4%	10.5%	8.8%	9.0%	

In an attempt to update the data from the 1993 study, I went to internet sources: *Handbook of International Economic Statistics, 1997*, www.odci.gov.cia/publications/hies97/h/tab79htm and www.stat-usa.gov. Using these sources, I was able get information on many economic indicators for the years through 1997. I have selected three which were compared in our 1993 study, Gross Domestic Product (GDP) which we called "Industrial Output" in the previous study, Inflation, and Unemployment. I chose another indicator of productivity, GDP Per Capita and an indicator of personal income, Average Monthly Wage, to include on this table for comparison. The data was incomplete for some countries, so only those with sufficient data are included.

years ago and put the old (reformed, calling themselves democratic socialists) communists back in power. Belarus, Bulgaria, Slovakia, Turkmenistan, and Uzbekistan have also gone backwards on the political spectrum. Belarus now has a Stalinist type president, Alexander Lukashenko, who intends to rule without reference to the elected parliament. He has kept Belarus in abject poverty and would close the borders to outsiders if he could. He recently forced the Soros Foundation out of Belarus because Mr. George Soros had been critical of his policies. Belarus may become like Romania under Ceausescu if this madman is not stopped.

We all know what has happened in the former Yugoslavia. The terrible civil war caused a breakup of the country in addition to resulting in 200,000 deaths. Why did this happen? Georgie Anne Geyer investigated the situation in 1992 and determined that the war was almost entirely brought about by the old communists, primarily Slobodan Milosovic and Radavan Karadic, as a way to prevent them from losing power. We heard of centuries old animosities that caused ethnic tensions, however, the different ethnic groups had lived together in peace and harmony through most of the years since the end of World War II. Then with the breakup of the Soviet Empire, long after the death of Marshall Tito who had held the different ethnic groups together by force, Milosovic and Karadic fomented enough ethnic hatred among the Serbs to cause them to go to war against the Croatians and Bosnians. Mrs. Geyer called the whole basis for the conflict, a "land grab" by the old communists.[8]

Across the Danube to the east, in Romania, conditions have changed more slowly than in such countries as Poland, The Czech Republic, and Hungary. These three countries voted in democratic governments after becoming independent in 1989 and relegated the old communists to second place (although two of them brought the old communists back later). Romania stuck with the old communists under Ion Iliescu from 1989 until November, 1996. At that time, the "Democratic Convention" won the largest number of seats in the parliament, and the leader of the Democratic Convention, Emil Constantinescu, was elected president, defeating Iliescu in a runoff election.

The seven years under Iliescu were not repressive, yet also were not what they could have been. While the old *Securitate* was disbanded and replaced by an organization called the SRI (Romanian Information Service), there was still an informer network in being, telephones being monitored and mail being opened. Who was doing it? Nobody in the government would admit that these actions were officially sanctioned, yet all Romanians knew they were taking place. Additionally, the old network of political police was still intact in 1997.

With sadness and regret, we can say that corruption took on such grandeur during the seven years that Iliescu was in power that the Romania was in danger to become another Iraq. While the economy was based on private property, the large Romanian owners came from the *nomenclatura*. Ordinary citizens are in danger of being oppressed again if the budding Mafia is not controlled.

The leaders of the Mafia became so very strong financially under Iliescu that President Constantinescu and the Parliament had a difficult fight to control them and to make the "rule of law" effective. Daily, in 1997, we learned of illegal maneuvers engaged in by the Mafia to obtain money by cheating the Romanian government, but nothing was done against them.

As related in Chapter 1, Ion Mihai Pacepa wrote a letter to Foreign Minister Adrian Severin in April, 1997, stating that unless Romania's "Political Police," the government informer network said to include one in ten Romanians, was disbanded, together with the connections that existed with the former KGB, Romania would have no chance of getting into NATO. Pacepa knew that the Political Police still existed. He had helped establish it thirty years before and knew it was still functioning even under the Constantinescu government.[9]

As we also said in Chapter 2, Severin took no action against the Political Police and Romania did not get into NATO. Other factors such as the poor progress in privatization as well as the continued existence of the Political Police can be blamed for Romania's lack of acceptance into NATO. In any case, the Romanian people appeared to be very disappointed. They thought that their application was valid: Romanian troops had been active in peace-keeping roles in Angola, Bosnia, and Albania. Romania's army is a solid institution. Romanians wanted NATO membership as another hedge against the Russians in case Yeltsin is succeeded by someone like Vladimir Zhirinofsky, or even worse, some of the old communists. Perhaps Adrian Severin was not the right person to tell that the Political Police must be disbanded. Severin, a member of Petre Roman's political party, had been an important member of the Iliescu government carried over by Constantinescu because Roman wanted the position for Severin as a price for joining the Democratic Convention in the coalition government.[10]

President Clinton made the decision to include Poland, The Czech Republic, and Hungary into NATO and to exclude Romania and Slovenia who had also made applications. In a surprise move, after the NATO meeting in Madrid in early July, 1997, when these acceptances and denials were made, President Clinton decided to visit Romania after his visit to Poland. On July 11, 1997, Air Force One touched down on Otopeni International Airport and President Clinton was on Romanian soil. He motored into Bucharest, spent a short visit to President Constantinescu's office in the Cotroceni Palace, and then went to *Piata Universitate*, the same location where the sit-in demonstration had taken place against Iliescu for fifty-nine days in 1990.

President Constantinescu gave a very stirring speech to the cheering crowd of 100,000 spectators in which he praised the good relations Romania and the U.S. are developing, promising to continue to develop democratic institutions in Romania. President Clinton then gave a rousing speech of encouragement. He first said that he was proud to be the first American president to visit a free Romania. He added, "No people- no people have suffered more under Communist repression. No people paid a higher price for the simple right to live in freedom."[11] Clinton then indicated that with the election of President Constantinescu, the dark days of communism are no more for Romania. He praised the country for the progress it had made since the previous November when Constantinescu took office, both economically and politically: "To all nations who embrace democracy and reform and wish to share the responsibilities of membership, I reaffirm from this plaza of freedom, the door to NATO is open. It will stay open, and we will help you walk through it."[12] He then encouraged the Romanians to stay the course of democracy and Romania would join NATO in two years.[13]

Among other problems faced by Romania, in the past four years, newspapers frequently exposed collusion between high government officials and businessmen. Bribery and corruption was rampant under Iliescu and is still occurring under Constantinescu. The stories of officials impounding rice imports from Vietnam and then selling the rice for their own enrichment, or Prime Minister Vacaroiu rejecting the highest bid for the Mangalia shipyards and giving it to a Korean firm (for a bribe) have been everyday news in *Romania Libera, Ziua, Cotdidianul,* and other newspapers, but little or no action has been taken against the perpetrators. The "Old Boy Network" of former communists kept the newspapers' revelations from becoming indictments.

At the same time, most of Romania's industrial capacity remained in the state owned industries where the guidelines were still, *"Timpul trece, leafa merge, noi cu drag muncim."* The work ethic of the employees in the state owned enterprises has been very poor, yet they continued to demand good salaries and job security. In August, 1997, Prime Minister Victor Ciorbea of the Democratic Convention announced the closing of seventeen large industrial dinosaurs, including three oil refineries. The news in the *Wall Street Journal* the next day included a statement that Romanian workers were protesting in the streets over the closings. The day after that, Prime Minister Ciorbia restated his intent to close the seventeen enterprises in spite of the protests.[14]

Is communism dead forever? Of course it is not, as we recognize its continued existence in China, Cuba, North Korea, and Vietnam. But is it dead in the newly independent states? Again, we have to say "No," because we know it has fostered a mafia-like group that is trying to retain the economic power formerly held by the communists and the communist system is still preferred by many older people who lived most of their lives under the it and fear that they will lose the security it gave them. British born educator Randall Baker saw this very early in his stay in Bulgaria. In discussing a national election, he related, "In rural areas, where communism had brought modest but measurable success, the Party still held sway."[15]

Croatian Slavenka Drakulic tells us, "The reality is that communism persists in the way people behave, in the looks on their faces, in the way they think. Despite the free elections and the celebrations of new democratic governments taking over in Prague, Budapest, and Bucharest, the truth is that people still go home to small, crowded apartments, drive unreliable cars, worry about their sickly children, do boring jobs, and eat poor quality food. The end of communism is still remote because communism, more than a political ideology or a method of government, is a state of mind..., that exorcising this way of being will take an unforeseeable length of time."[16]

Unfortunately, these ordinary, non-political people are not the only adherents to the discredited communist system. President Alexander Lukashenko in Belarus would return to Stalinist communism if he could. He may be able to after Boris Yeltsin retires from the Presidency of Russia in the year 2000 (if his health will allow him to serve that long). Slobodan Milosovic in the diminished Yugoslav federation has tried to reverse democratic elections that reduce his power. He would reimpose communism in Yugoslavia to protect his position. His colleague and fellow war criminal in Bosnia, Radavan Karadic would bring back communism in Bosnia to be able to return to power.

There are many other opportunists in the world, particularly in the newly independent states, who are biding their time, waiting for economic hard times or ethnic conflicts to emerge which can give them a basis for coming forth to lead their people out of the problem. If they do so in the name of Marxism-Leninism, and are successful, their subjects are in for dictatorship, repression, isolation, and deprivation. Communism cannot exist in an "open society."[17] It must hide its failures and lie to everyone saying that it is creating a wonderful life for them. Instead, it is creating a wonderful life for a restricted group of thugs and "yes men" around the chief dictator, while, everyone else suffers deprivations of freedom and the means to sustain life.

Let us not quickly forget the terrible life of repression and deprivation endured by so many millions of unfortunate people who had to live under communism from 1917 to 1989, and the millions who still live under it. The democratic countries won the "Cold War," but communism still exists and must be further discredited. We cannot live in compete comfort and security until all of the societies of the earth are Open societies.

Notes

1. Marcel Cornis-Pope, *The Unfinished Battles: Romanian Postmodernism Before and After 1989*, (Iasi, Romania: Polirom Co. S.A., 1996), p. 13.
2. Vladimir Tismaneau, *Reinventing Politics: Eastern Europe from Stalin to Havel*, (New York: Free Press, 1992), p. 249.
3. Slavenka Drakulic, *How We Survived Communism and Even Laughed*, (New York: W.W. Norton & Company, 1991), p. xi.

4.   Slavenka Drakulic, *How We Survived Communism and Even Laughed*, (New York: Harper Perennial, 1993), pp. 195-196.

5.   Slavenka Drakulic, *Cafe Europa: Life After Communism* (New York: W.W. Norton and Company, 1997), p. 319.

6.   Andrei Codrescu, *Zombification: Stories from NPR*, (New York: St. Martin's Press, 1994), p. 197.

7.   McCollum, J.K. and M. Gentle-Marsh, "Privatization in Eight Former Socialist Countries of Eastern Europe," *International Journal of Public Administration* 18 (No. 6, 1995), pp. 973-974.

8.   Georgie Anne Geyer, Speech to the Annual Fulbright Association Meeting, Washington, D.C., September 23, 1992.

9.   "Pacepa Calls for Dissolution of Political Police," *Ziua*, (April 30, 1997), p. 1.

10.   One of the weaknesses of the Constantinescu-Ciorbea government is "coalition strife." This problem is mentioned in *The Economist* 344 (August 23, 1997) p. 40: "The ruling Democratic Convention, which shares power with two other parties, is itself a grouping of several parties...The other main member of the coalition, (is) the Social Democratic Union of Petre Roman. If Mr. Ciorbea is crushed between the IMF and the populace, Mr. Roman would shed few tears."

11.   *Weekly Compilation of Presidential Documents* 33, No. 29 (July 21, 1997) p. 1061.

12.   Ibid., p. 1062.

13.   Author's note: "I was in the crowd that day, but it was impossible to take notes because of the crush of the crowd. I am reporting what I remember. Both speeches were in the speakers' native tongue and a translator then translated as the speakers paused after each sentence. They were very appreciative of the Clinton visit. Looking around, I was struck by the youth of its participants. Easily ninety-five percent were less than forty years old."

14.   "Postscripts," *Wall Street Journal*, August 17 and 18, 1997, p. A-9 and "Still on Track: Romania," *The Economist* 344 (August 23, 1997) p. 40.

15.   Randall Baker, *Summer in the Balkans: Laughter and Tears After Communism*, West Hartford, CT: Kumarian Press, 1994, p. 12.

16.   Slavenka Drakulic, *How We Survived Communism and Even Laughed*, (New York: Harper Perennial, 1993), pp. xvi-xvii.

17.   "Why an Open Society?" is asked in the literature of the Soros Foundations for an Open Society. "A *closed society* is the creation of a totalitarian regime: everything must come from the state-ideas, initiatives, financing, everything must be controlled by the state. Individuals have no active role in the development of society: they expect or wait for things to be done for them and paid for by the state. This does not help a society to grow: it suppresses creativity in the name of control and order. After the fall of communism, this had to change. But how? In which direction?

An *open society* is a democratic society. Citizens take an active part in the development of their country. Their creativity, ideas and strength are used to the benefit of the entire society. The country is open to the flow of information, to understanding different cultures, to debating important controversial issues before the latter become a source of conflict. This is what open societies should be and how closed societies need to be transformed. Prospectus, *Soros Foundation for an Open Society Romania,* Fifth Anniversary, 1995, pp. 2-3.

Chapter 9
Some Ideas for Newly Independent Citizens

In the past eight years, many programs have been initiated to help the newly independent states transition into democracy and free market conditions. The Fulbright program was not new, since it was begun in 1947, but it was expanded in the decade of the nineties to send more academics into Russia, the CIS, and Eastern Europe. For many of us, this was just the beginning of the challenge. We found some other programs that allowed us to try to increase the knowledge of free market management and democracy.

One such program was the internship program initiated in 1991 by the U.S. Information Agency (USIA) under the name. "Central and Eastern European Training Program (CEETP). It specified that U.S. institutions could apply for U.S. government support to bring individuals from central and eastern Europe who were working in the areas of local government/public administration, communications/news media, and business administration to the U.S. for a four to ten week internship to learn about operating in democratic/free market conditions.

We sent a proposal to USIA in 1993 to bring eight Romanian managers to the Huntsville, Alabama area for a five-week internship in local businesses. Our USIA proposal was not funded, but we used a similar proposal to get funds from the Soros Foundation for an Open Society[1] for recruiting assistance, air fare, and medical insurance to bring five Romanian managers to Huntsville. At that time, we were able to get additional support from two Rotary Clubs, three local businesses, Disk Manufacturing, Inc., Ryder

International, Inc. a SCI Systems, Inc., and the University of Alabama in Huntsville to support the intern program. We had the interns, two ladies and three men, ranging in age from 32 to 51, in Huntsville from late February through early April, 1994. Initially, we gave them a one week orientation at the university and some local institutions such as the newspaper, Chamber of Commerce, Small Business Development Center, county court house, and several local businesses. We then placed them into one of the three local businesses (all three at this time were manufacturing businesses) for a four week internship. The interns and the mentors for the interns in the businesses reported that the effort was very worthwhile and should be repeated.

Following that experience, we were able to get contracts from the USIA to bring 24 interns to Huntsville in 1995 and 24 in 1996. We again had some of the support from the Soros Foundation, some from UAH, and some from local businesses. In 1995, we placed interns for four weeks with ADS Environmental Services, Inc., Avex, Inc., Coyne Cylinder, Inc., Engelhard Corp., The Fulcrum Group, Inc., Mevatec Corp., Onan Corp., Pentastar Electronics, Inc., Rite Way, Inc, Sparta, Inc., Shamrock Sportsbag Inc., SRS Technologies, Inc., Wyle Laboratories, Inc., and the University of Alabama in Huntsville. In 1996, we had interns with Adtran, Inc., Engineered Plastics Co., Inc., Fastec, Inc., Fast Word, Inc., Fulcrum Group, Inc., Huntsville Hospital, *Huntsville Times,* Merrill Lynch, Inc., Pacific-America-Asia, Inc., Quinn Enterprises, Inc., Scitek, Inc., Sparta, Inc., Thompson Plastics Co., Inc, Universal Construction Company, Inc., and the University of Alabama in Huntsville. The results seemed to be very worthwhile to the interns and we hoped that they were sharing their knowledge from the internship with other managers when they returned from Romania. We also hoped that they were impressed with the openness of our American society and would try to influence their countrymen to be active in the political processes and elect people who would improve the live of Romanians.[2] The feedback obtained at a reunion with forty-two of the former interns in May, 1997, indicated that some improvement in knowledge, skills, and managerial ability did seem to be present with former interns that was not as prevalent with a small control group. These results are found in Appendix A, "Effectiveness of Management Internships: The Romanian Experience," which was a paper presented to the American Society of Business and Behavioral Sciences in February,

1998.

We had heard many complaints about governmental actions from Romanians sitting in our seminars in Romania. When we would advocate that they write letters to the President or the legislators, they would say, "Oh, no, we would never do that." "Why?" we would ask. "Because nobody would pay any attention to us," or "They do not want to listen to us. They have been elected to office and they think they can do anything they want to." Some people even said, "We don't want to be run over by a truck."

Obviously, democracy does not exist in their beliefs as it exists in the beliefs of most Americans. We are not reluctant to tell our elected representatives what we think and that they have voted incorrectly if we think they have. Romanians have a very different perspective, little divorced from the "divine right" theory, that anyone who has a position of authority cannot be taken to task for his or her actions and decisions. They feel that the citizen who individually complains may get into trouble with the government, or with the shady "power behind the government."

We had these reactions from Romanians from 1991 through 1997. In 1996, we spent eight months in the beautiful medieval city of Sibiu at the Lucian Blaga University. Sibiu is in the heart of the Transylvanian region of Romania and the outlook of its people was different from the Bucharest area. The people seemed to be somewhat more progressive than Romanians in other areas, yet they also displayed a despair of trying to change anything in the Iliescu government.

Because of our perceptions of the need to open the society, at one point while we were in Sibiu, we wrote a series of letters to the Romanian people. It was our hope that the letters would be translated into Romanian and widely published in the newspapers. This did not happen during the stay in Sibiu because I wanted them published anonymously (I wasn't sure of my USIA program director's acceptance of my freelance ideas), but when we returned to Huntsville and brought 24 Romanian intern-managers in September and October, 1996, we gave copies of the letters to the interns and they were very enthusiastic about the ideas they contained. On their own initiative, some of the interns translated the letters and sent their translations to Romanian newspapers where they were published just before the October and November, 1996 elections. These elections were won by the Democratic Convention and finally a change away from Iliescu and the old communists took place.

While we have no illusions that the letters brought about any changes of attitude of Romanian voters, the interns who read and translated them were excited by their message and voluntarily did the work of translation and sending them to Romanian newspapers. We never recommended such actions, nor did we try to keep the interns from taking these actions. The letters contain some ideas that they thought were important for other Romanians to share, so why shouldn't they be able to send these ideas back to Romania?

We know of at least four newspapers that published the letters and one website that presents a copy of the letters.[3] The six letters are reproduced below:

An Open Letter to the Romanian People

Dear Romanian People,

You may ask, "Who is this foreigner who thinks he can tell us anything about our country? Let me tell you of my knowledge of Romania. In the past five years, I have come to Romania twelve times for visits ranging between two weeks and eleven months in duration. In all, I have spent twenty-one months in your beautiful country, talking with your people and living among your citizens.

My name is James, born in a small city (3,000 population) in a midwestern state in the United States of America. I was educated in the American public schools through high school, attained a degree in engineering at a military academy, a masters degree in political science at a Catholic University, a masters degree in public administration at a city university, and a doctor of philosophy degree in business administration at a state university. I served in the U.S. Army in Germany and in South Vietnam, in addition to some places in the U.S. I worked for a time as a manager, and have taught in American Universities for twenty-two years.

In September, 1991, I came to Romania as a Fulbright Scholar. I was the first American professor to be assigned to teach management classes at the Academy of Economic Studies in Bucharest. Additionally, I taught two and four hour seminar courses for the Romanian Management Institute (IROMA) in locations all over Romania: Bacau, Braila, Brasov, Calarasi, Cluj, Piriul Rece, Ploiesti, Sibiu, and Suceava in addition to Bucharest. I stayed in

Romania for eleven months and wrote most of a business management book during that time, *Idei Americane Pentru Manageri Romani* (American Ideas for Romanian Managers). Since then, I have returned to Romania for research and teaching on numerous occasions: two weeks in December, 1992; two weeks in June, 1993; three weeks in August and September, 1993; two weeks in December, 1993; four weeks in June, 1994; two weeks in August, 1994; two weeks in December, 1994; one week in March, 1995; five weeks in July and August, 1995; two weeks in October, 1995; and now for seven months in 1996. I have taught courses in strategic management at Costinesti and Mangalia and organized business workshops in Bucharest. Since January, 1996, I have been a visiting professor at the Lucian Blaga University in Sibiu.

In early 1994, I had five Romanian managers in my home city of Huntsville, Alabama, for a five week internship in American companies. I had twenty-four Romanian managers in American companies or working with my university during five week internships in early 1995. I helped restart the Bucharest Rotary Club in May, 1992, and arranged to have Romania's first Rotary Ambassadorial Scholar come to the University of Alabama in Huntsville in 1995. Additionally, I have had two other Romanian visitors come to Huntsville at my invitation.

With all of this exposure to Romanians, I should know you very well. I know you well enough to say that I admire you greatly and want you to improve your lives, but I still do not know you well. I need to know your language better, and to understand your culture better. Forgive me when I make mistakes when I recommend something to you, because I come from a different background. Never-the-less, I do want to recommend some things to you.

First and foremost, you Romanian citizens are now living in a representative democracy. You chose the government that makes and executes your laws. The members of that government are your servants. I don't think you understand that and the members of your government don't understand it either. You should make this government be responsible to you, the citizens, instead of feeling that the government is a "sovereign" over you. It is you, the Romanian people, who are "sovereign." The government exists to serve you and to perform services for you that you yourselves cannot perform. You must choose your representatives carefully and everyone should be involved in the electoral process. It is your responsibility to investigate what the political candidates stand for and to vote for those who best represent your beliefs.

Too often, I have heard Romanians (and people in other countries, including my own) say, "It doesn't matter what I think or whether I vote. The government will do what it wants to do anyway." No! No! That is not true. You are responsible for what is happening and for what the government is doing. As your national anthem tells you, "Wake Up, Romania!" Accept your responsibility to make the government govern in ways that will bring well-being to its citizens and an improvement in Romania's reputation in the world.
Your friend,
James

Letter Number 2

Dear People of Romania,

Why wasn't the communist system able to sustain itself? Have you ever asked yourself this question? With all of its marvelous promises of equality for all in a "Democratic Republic," what went wrong? It went wrong because it was not a "natural" system. Natural systems evolve in response to the felt needs of society. The monarchy was a natural system because it was brought about by the will of the people who had decided that they needed a wise, benevolent administrator to guide the affairs of state through perilous times. King Carol the first certainly fulfilled that desire of the people by winning independence for Romania in the war with Turkey in 1878 and by establishing a more modern society than had existed before, using his wealth to build many public buildings and attracting foreign investors who built Romania's railroads and some of its industry.

King Ferdinand continued this tradition through the desperate years of World War I which ultimately gave Romania the landholdings with Romanian people that had been controlled by other nations. Queen Marie worked unceasingly for the Romanian people during the war and afterward to help Romania get what it rightly deserved. King Carol II did not have an admirable personal life, but the institution of the monarchy maintained a strong nation right into World War II when King Michael was the monarch.

In all of the years of the monarchy, the Romanian people were satisfied with the government. How then did the monarchy fall? Through imposition by military power of a false, unnatural form of government: communism. Communism was never openly accepted by any nation. It was always imposed by military might. It happened in Russia, in all of the Soviet Republics, in all of the Eastern European nations, in China, in North Korea, in Laos, in Cambodia, and in Cuba. In no country was communism chosen by the votes of the people.

What happened in each of these nations where communism was imposed by military force? This wonderful "democratic" system quickly became a repressive dictatorship. Elections only carried the name of the current dictator and his approved clique. Was there ever a communist dictator who voluntarily relinquished power? Maybe a few in 1989 in Eastern Europe when it was apparent that the failed communist system was falling apart. But think of the majority of communist leaders: Stalin - died while still holding power, Mao Tse-tung - died while still holding the reins of power, Kim Il Sung - died while still holding the reins of power, Ceausescu - executed two days after trying to escape from the country. Wouldn't the same fate have come to most of the communist dictators who ruled at the same time as Ceausescu if they had tried voluntarily to give up their power? Probably, because they had engaged in so many outrageous acts against their own citizens that the others, too, would have been put on trial and executed if they had tried to live on as retired dictators. We don't seem to have many examples of retired dictators: Hitler committed suicide, Idi Amin had to flee from Uganda, Saddam Hussein can't give up in Iraq or that will be the end of him.

So what did we have under communism? A system that promised equality and was forced onto society by dictatorial power. Yes, there was some leveling of the opportunities for average people, while an elite security force around the dictator lived in luxury. But let's examine the "leveling" for the masses. Communism discouraged creativity. Many of the best and the brightest members of society escaped to other countries so that they could safely be creative. Most of them found welcoming arms in truly democratic countries which were able to use their talents to enrich the receiving countries. The "brain drain" from communist countries was a great benefit for the United States, United Kingdom, France, Canada, and other democratic countries.

Communism also destroyed the sense of private property and made everyone indifferent to the importance of ownership. When "everybody owns everything," the reality is that nobody owns anything and nobody cares about anything. Producers were able to put shoddy products into the markets knowing that the consumers in communist countries had no choice but to buy what they produced. Fulfilling their quotas became the goal of manufacturers and there was no concern for the buyers. After all, the factory managers were not rewarded for pleasing indigenous customers, they were rewarded for fulfilling the quotas that had been set by communist party bureaucrats sitting in the capital who had no conception of what the right goals should be other than that of pleasing the dictator.

Communism also damaged the educational system. Every pupil knew from the first form (grade) that there was no reason to work hard to obtain knowledge and qualifications. Graduates were placed in jobs without proper qualifications. The teachers had no concern for the education of the children: students were not allowed to fail and thus they might not know anything as they progressed from form to form and finally matriculated. For the first ten years of school, there was no competition. A student could be as stupid as a pig or as clever as a philosopher and it made no difference. After the tenth form, some students would be put into a three year trade school for electricians, bricklayers, etc., and often emerge not knowing their trade. The others who went on to the universities did encounter competition and were assigned to work situations around the country based on their marks: the highest in Bucharest, second highest in other cities, and lower performers in the towns and villages. Nobody had any choice in their assignments unless they were connected to high party officials.

Eventually, the paranoia in Romania was so great that the country was virtually isolated from the non-communist outside world. Foreign influences were limited by keeping Romanians at home and keeping them from talking to foreigners in Romania. The party's rationale: "Smart people will gain information and try to make us change something - this will cause trouble." The communists hastened the downfall of their own system by closing the borders. The people now know too much to ever allow communism to come back. Closing yourself off from the rest of the world ensures that you go backward and your government becomes repressive in trying to justify its obtuse actions. Thus communism killed itself. It was a false system that did not deserve to exist in the first place. Let us all thank God that communism is dead in Romania. But let us be on our guard that it is never resurrected.
Your friend,

James
Letter Number 3
Dear People of Romania:

You are special people on the earth. No other nation is like the Romanian nation. Its people are unique, highly intelligent, capable of achieving great feats of creativity, and of surviving great deprivations. You have demonstrated that you can individually attain marvelous results. Those lucky individuals who are able to be educated at universities ingest the knowledge presented to them as well or better than scholars anywhere else in the world. Your workers who do not go to the universities work hard and provide well for themselves in spite of the hardships of the transition economy.

Romania has riches that many other countries envy. You have wonderful agricultural lands, great mineral wealth, marvelous natural attractions for tourists, and a large space for your twenty-three million people. In short, Romania has all of the necessary ingredients for greatness except one: organization. If all of your space, resources, and your marvelous population were properly organized, Romania would be a great power among the family of nations. You would not necessarily have great military power, but it's not important for an individual nation to have great military power today if you are allied with powerful, democratic friends. Other kinds of power are more important for you: economic power, cultural power, diplomatic power, educational power.

Romania can have these powers. Why doesn't it have these powers now? The more than forty years of communism are greatly to blame for the less-than-ideal state of affairs that exists today. Communism was imposed upon you after World War II without your consent, without the King's consent: it was forced on you by the military power of the Soviet Union. Why did it happen? One answer is that your Romanian army forces accompanied and fought beside the armies of the German Third Reich in their invasion of the Soviet Union in 1941. Your armies were part of the force that surrounded Stalingrad in 1943. Your armies fought bravely in a cause that we all came to believe in - the defeat of Godless communism, although your ally at that time, Nazi Germany, was not acceptable.

In retrospect, we Americans are not proud of the decisions made at Yalta that put all of the nations that became Soviet "satellites" behind the "Iron Curtain." Did the Soviet Union deserve such benefits from being one of the victorious allies after World War II? Not in my opinion. After taking Bessarabia and part of Bukovina away from Romania, the Soviet Union invaded Finland in 1939 simply because it had gotten these three regions within its sphere of influence as a result of the Molotov-Ribbentrop Pact. When the Soviet armies first invaded Finland, both Great Britain and France came very close to declaring war on the Soviet Union. President Roosevelt of the U.S. wrote a disapproving letter to the President of the Soviet Union. Later, when the Germans invaded Poland from the west, Soviet armies invaded Poland from the east. What kind of ally was that for Britain, France, and the United States to embrace as a brother-in-arms? We did it in our zeal to defeat Hitler, considering naziism as a worse evil than communism. Yes, Hitler had to be defeated, but we gave too much to Stalin.

During World War II, the United States shipped hundreds of thousands of artillery guns, tanks, jeeps, warplanes, and even locomotives and rail cars to the Soviet Union. Without our help, Hitler would have triumphed against the Soviet armies. What did we get for our generous support of the Soviet Union? An intractable, lifetime enemy. Despite our assistance, Stalin blamed us for making his forces fight alone and suffer twenty million deaths (which interestingly is about the same number of deaths caused by Stalin's purges in the 1930's). Did Stalin deserve to control Poland, Czechoslovakia, Hungary, Bulgaria, Albania, and Romania by virtue of being on the winning side? Not at all. Our only excuse for giving so much to the evil communist dictator was that we were weary of war in 1945 and wanted to go back to a peaceful life.

So you, dear Romanian people, fell into the sphere of influence of the "evil empire" of Joseph Stalin. Badly misguided Romanians carried out the imposition of the communist system in Romania. Unfortunately, after the abject failure of communism that culminated in your revolution in 1989, some of the residual effects of the communist system remain.

One aspect is the inclination toward central authority. Under the communist system, all citizens were supposed to be equal. Were they? Of course not. The opinions of individual citizens were not considered at all. People were told how to think by t
heir "glorious, all knowing" leader. All decisions, great and small, important and trivial, had to be put before him for his approval. Is it logical that one person should be making decisions about moving

business offices or acquiring tractors for any particular collective farm? Of course not. Such centralization is ridiculous. The managers closest to the activity should be allowed to make such decisions. However, this tendency for centralization still persists in state owned enterprises.

Let us look at some of the other bad effects of communism. Under communism, private property was not allowed. Without private property, incentives to use property in the best ways do not exist. When the government told you, "everything is owned by the people," didn't it really mean, "Nothing is owned by the people."? Nobody took care of "commonly owned property." State appointed managers tried to make their enterprises work well, but efficiency was not an important criterion.

One of the worst untruths that was propagated by the communist regime was that all citizens were equal in all respects. We know that a ruling class of party officials lived very well under the communist system when average citizens struggled to put any kind of food on their tables. High party officials were not destined to eat in the "food factories" devised by Ceausescu in the last year of his dictatorship. Everyone was not equal then, nor are they now. Each person brings to world his or her own specialties and abilities. Some have much ability, some have less. Now with a democracy, the equality that is available is that of opportunity. Everyone should be able to try to do anything that is legal to succeed in life.

Your friend,
James

Letter Number 4

Dear People of Romania,

Let's talk about some good news! *You* are in *command* of *your destiny*. How can that be? It is because you are citizens of a country with an elected, democratic form of government. You are electing representatives to speak for you every time you vote in an election and these representatives speak for you in making the laws you want. If they vote for legislation you don't like, you can tell them they are not properly representing you and you can work for their defeat in the next election. Of course, you will not agree with every decision they make for you and some of them are relatively unimportant and don't deserve any overt action on your part. However, if they are far off from your ideas of how this country should be run, you should speak out and let your representatives know that they are not pleasing you.

I have spoken to Romanians on several occasions and heard their complaints against the government's actions. I would then advocate that the unhappy citizens call or write to their legislators or to the President to tell them of your discontent. The citizens would then say, "Oh, no, we would never do that!" "Why not?" I would ask. They would say that nobody would pay any attention to them, or worse, they would say that the senator or deputy would take retribution against them for speaking up. I couldn't believe my ears! These representatives would punish citizens for disagreeing with them? Surely, that cannot be true. Those legislators and the President are the servants of the Romanian people and if they have any idea of punishing a voter for disagreeing with them, they don't belong in any elected body. They have a false image of their true position in the hierarchy of a democratic society.

You, the Romanian *people* are on top, the sovereign body that the government must serve and answer to. If individuals choose to represent a portion of that sovereign body, then they subordinate their existence to the service of that constituency. In some instances, they may not vote the way *Domnul* (Mr.) X or Group Y wants them to vote, or may oppose the point of view of *Domnul* Z of Group A within their constituency, because each representative is serving a large group of citizens and the majority of those citizens agrees with the representative and not these individuals or groups, but they still should take notice of the dissenting ideas.

The legislators should be deciding and voting in the ways that the majority of their constituency believes is right, but at the same time, they had better be listening to minority opinions and recognizing that other ideas are being expressed. And the legislator should never, ever remotely consider punishing anyone for expressing and opinion that conflicts with the legislator's opinion. The majority decides, but minority rights must be observed.

Too often, the legislation that is created seems to be made in a vacuum. Nobody knew that an issue was under consideration until it had been voted into law and then it was too late to express an opposing position. Actually, the legislation is made in the open and newsmen are reporting on the issues being debated every day. It is the responsibility of citizens to read the newspapers and keep themselves informed of what the President, Parliament, and lower legislative bodies such as city councils or *judet* (county) councils are discussing. Even if some disagreeable legislation goes through and is signed into law and you find fault with it, you should still complain to your elected representatives. They will then know of your discontent and if enough of you are unhappy, they will change the law.

I have written to my two senators, my congressman in the House of Representatives, and to the President of the United States on numerous occasions. In almost all cases, I have received a letter in reply explaining why the government representative disagreed with me, or in cases where I was advocating some action that hadn't happened yet, what their position on the issue was at that time. In several instances, my views ultimately prevailed. Of course, it wasn't my views alone, but those held by many fellow citizens who were similarly inspired to write to express their opinions and these opinions helped form the basis of the position taken by the representative.

Has anything bad ever happened to me for expressing my ideas to a congressional person or the President? Of course not. They always thank me for expressing my views and for being interested in the activities of the government.

Besides individual actions to influence the President or the legislators, there are other ways that are even more effective to influence them by supporting lobbying groups that represent your ideas to government representatives. Bodies such as chambers of commerce, labor unions, employer associations, professional associations, religious groups, cultural groups, political parties, consumer groups, and many others may present opinions to representatives which have the weight of the many members behind them. You probably don't have all of these bodies in being in Romania yet, but you will have them soon. They are valuable sources of public opinion and the legislators pay attention to what they believe.

I think that much of what I am saying is contrary to the thinking of many of you at this time. Forty years of dictatorship has conditioned you to staying inside a shell when it comes to political activities. But a new day has dawned! This new day is the time of the *people*! It is a time for all of you to take an interest in your future and make your influence known to your servants in the governing bodies of Romania.

It has been said of some of the worst periods of history that the greatest tragedy was that good people stood aside and did nothing to correct the wrong directions being taken by misguided leaders. Hitler remilitarized the Rhineland in 1936 in contravention to the Treaty of Versailles and Britain and France did nothing. Hitler occupied the Sudetenland of Czechoslovakia and Britain's Prime Minister Chamberlain, France's Premier Daladier, and the German generals did nothing, even though many of them foresaw at that time that Hitler was leading Germany to eventual ruin. What would have happened if some courageous groups had stood up to Hitler in one of these foolhardy actions and "called his bluff?" Several historians believe that Hitler would have been deposed in the face of determined opposition and the course of history would have been very different. There would have been no World War II in the way that we experienced it with 250 million deaths.

What would that have meant for Romania? No communist "iron curtain," no Soviet occupation, and continued prosperity for the Romanian people under a constitutional monarchy. These outcomes are much more attractive than the ones that actually took place.

Of course, we cannot rewrite history, but we can make a point that good citizens should make their voices heard and keep the leaders form making poor decisions, or if poor decisions are made, to try to get the leaders to correct themselves. Individual citizens are not in the momentous positions occupied by people like Prime Minister Chamberlain, Premier Daladier, or the German Generals, but they can have a strong impact on decisions leaders make if they will take a proper interest and express themselves to their representatives.

My warmest regards,
James

Letter Number 5

Dear Romanian People,

This "time of transition" is difficult for all of you. You have more opportunities than before, but many people are losing their buying power because of inflation. More money is coming in, but it buys less than before. What is the answer for this problem? If I knew, I would be a highly paid consultant for your government.

But first, let's look on the bright side. You have all kinds of food and consumer goods in the stores which were not available to you in 1989. Your markets abound with goods that either were produced by Romanian producers or imported from foreign producers. When you are ready to buy something, you usually have lots of choices for your purchase. How has this change come about? It has happened because private businesses are willing to take risks to buy foods and other goods in the belief that they can make a profit by offering them for sale to you.

When a new private business begins, it is a cause for celebration. The owner or owners believe enough in Romania that they are willing to risk their money to create a business that serves customer's needs. If the business is successful, the owner makes a profit and both consumers and owners are happy. That is, everyone should be happy. Often, however, there are problems in this transition economy that greatly affect private businesses and need to be addressed.

This transition economy is a "mixed economy." There are privately owned businesses and state owned businesses operating at the same time and often in the same business, so they are competing against each other. The competition between private companies and state companies is usually unfair for several reasons. First, the state pays the wages of the state-owned companies and they don't have the need to be efficient. State-owned companies cannot go bankrupt, so their managers are not under as much pressure to perform well as are managers of private companies.[4] This usually allows state-owned companies to have lower prices than private companies must charge. Usually, this is not a major problem and privately owned companies attract customers because they provide better service.

But let's look at how the government treats the private companies. Businesses are subject to a large number of inspections from the government. Inspections come from the Fire Prevention inspectors, tax inspectors, Public Space inspectors, economic police inspectors, veterinary inspectors, League for Protection of Customers inspectors, Department of Finance and Pricing inspectors, Sanitary Police inspectors, and others. In a city like Bucharest, there may be inspectors from three levels of government inspecting the same activity: national, city, and sector (precinct). The inspectors come at different times and a business may pass its sanitation inspection from the national inspectors one day and fail the city's sanitation inspection the next. The fine charged for the violation will be just as large from the city as it would have been from the national inspector and the efforts to correct the perceived violation is just as disruptive.

Do state-owned businesses get the same amount of attention as private businesses? Private owners are convinced that they do not and it is logical that they would not. Why would the state fine itself? It may inspect state-owned firms, but simply gives advice to state managers rather than taking a heavy handed approach with fines and threats to close down the business that happens with private businesses. Is this fair? Of course not and it has driven private businessmen to decide to leave Romania rather than continue fighting under such an unfair system.

In this time of transition, private businesses should be encouraged rather than discouraged. We look forward to a time when the state-owned businesses are privatized and competing with other private businesses under the same conditions. These conditions that favor the state-owned firms should be eliminated. Instead, the Parliament seems to believe that there is not enough regulation of private businesses as they pass more and more laws that restrict the private businesses' ability to operate. It is almost as though there is a private war between the government and private businesses. This condition reflects the old, centralized mentality that existed before 1989.

The new mentality should recognize that the private sector is Romania's most progressive institution and will do more good than any other to improve the standard of living for Romanians. State-owned firms should be privatized quickly. Parliament should review all of the restrictive legislation it has created and which was previously created and is still being enforced with a view to eliminating much of this legislation.[5]

I have heard high level government officials say, "We have too many laws. Some go back to the time of the monarchy, some to the communist era, and some passed since the communist era. Nobody knows what laws apply anymore." Apparently, these many, many inspectors of private business think that they know what laws apply. They make it very difficult for private businesses to stay in business. Let's give these inspectors something else to do, like researching all of the laws in their field of inspection and recommending the elimination of the ones that don't apply anymore (and force them to find laws that should be eliminated).

Romania needs a strong private sector more than it needs intrusive legislation. The taxes from private businesses in a strong private sector will pay the government's bills in the future. If the private sector stays weak, who will pay the bill? The state-owned companies? Don't bet on it.

Your friend,

James

Letter Number 6

Dear People of Romania,

Let me say a few words about some writers of the past who discussed the role of government in relation to the citizens. Maybe you have heard of them: Thomas Hobbes and John Locke. Hobbes, writing in the 17th century, was about one hundred years before Locke. In his study of government, which he named "Leviathon" which means whale, he developed a line of reasoning for why governments exist. He looked at human beings in the natural state, that is, without any controls over their actions. In the natural state as perceived by Hobbes, people act selfishly. They have no regard at all for their fellow human beings and are continually fighting among themselves for the best food, the best habitations, the best mates.

Since there are no rules to live by, they take what they want by destroying other human beings who have something that they want. There is no penalty for clubbing your neighbor to death because you want the antelope he has killed for food, the cave that he has found for himself, or for his wife who is devoted to him. Hobbes sees life in such conditions as "brutish, nasty, and short." Because of such brutal conditions, people have instituted government to provide rules and police forces that will prevent the strong from dominating the weak and the greed from stealing from anyone who is not able to protect their property.

There is much truth to be found in this reason for government. If human beings are not given some codes of behavior, many will unfairly dominate others. Certainly, we need a ruling body that prevents those who simply have the most "brute strength" from dominating others. Government requires that people act together in a society to establish what the rules for living should be, such as rules for property ownership, rules for commerce, rules for social relationships, etc. We have to agree that government is good so long as it does not go too far with its "police powers" and tries to intrude on the civil liberties of individuals. All citizens should have the right to enjoy their lives so long as they don't interfere with other's lives and should have the right to enjoy the property they accumulate fairly within the rules accepted by the society. Of course they have to support the government by paying taxes to provide salaries for those who make and enforce the laws and for the facilities that are required for government functioning.

All is well so long as the government officials recognize that the reason for their existence is to serve society and not that society exists to serve the government. This latter idea prevailed in the time of "absolute monarchies" and dictatorships that have existed from time to time, but ultimately destroy themselves, but in the process, destroy the lives of many innocent citizens.

The other writer, John Locke, wrote his most famous work, "Two Treatises on Government" about one hundred years after Hobbes wrote "Leviathon." Locke also looked at humans in the natural state without government or laws. In his view, humans are mostly good in their nature and have "right reasoning powers" that help them make the proper decisions in dealing with other human beings. Locke recognized, however, that a small proportion of any group will not exercise right reasoning and will make life inconvenient for others. They will use brute strength to dominate those with less strength and will scheme and plot to steal and destroy what others have earned by their hard work.

Because of this small minority that makes life inconvenient for the majority, governments are instituted to establish rules to control the lawless minority. This is the argument for 'limited government" and not a government that tries to control all activities of the citizens. Under the Hobbesian scheme, unless a law specifically allows an action to take place, it isn't allowed. Under the Lockean ideas, actions are allowed unless a law specifically prohibits it.

Laws are, of course, instituted in modern societies to provide safe methods for driving on the streets and for making merchants be truthful in selling the products that they say they are selling and not shoddy products. Even in Lockean 'limited governments' of today, laws are very extensive. They do not, however, intrude on the civil liberties of citizens - those allowing them to make a living for themselves by taking initiative and acting fairly with their fellow citizens, of allowing them to speak out against the existing government to try to make it change its makeup and ways of ruling on cases arising out of controversies over how to interpret the laws. They do not engage in listening to conversations between private citizens.

These ideas about government should be known by all citizens of a democratic nation. They should understand the reasons why governments exist, but insist that governmental power should be limited. Government officials are servants of the entire population and they must recognize that they serve their constituency. They must accept that they are limited in authority and do not have absolute power over their bosses, the people who elected them. I hope these ideas are interesting to you and helpful in improving your understanding in this time of transition.

Your true friend,

James

A Bright, Democratic Future

We hope that the message of these letters was a message for the citizens of all countries which were under communist governments for forty-five years, or more. The letters, written in mid-1996 and published in October, 1996, may now be obsolete in some aspects for Romanians. The Constantinescu government, elected in November, 1996, is trying to open the economy, privatize more state-owned enterprises, and be more responsive to the electorate. Yet, much more needs to be accomplished. Many scandals were still being publicized in the Romanian news media in mid-1997 with little movement toward correcting the serious inequities.

A non-government owned television station known as "Pro TV" now gives unbiased news to the Romanian people who have cable hookups and seems to be very popular with them. Cable viewers also have programs from other parts of the world: NBC (U.S.), Skynews (U.K.), Euronews (Belgium), plus programs in German, French, Italian, and Spanish. There is also a plethora of newspapers covering all of the political spectrum. The problem still exists, however, that the uncovered political scandals do not result in any reversal of action or punishment of the implicated miscreants. Perhaps this will change if the Democratic Convention gains a stronger position in the country. Progress is being made in privatizing state owned enterprises, but as conditions now stand, the old communist legacy is still affecting Romanians, both in their collective mindset and in the economic success they are having. An imperative is that of complete eradication of the "political police." Another is that of eliminating the tampering of the mail. A third is the need for prosecution of former officials who have misused government properties.

Much of what pertains to Romania also pertains to the other former communist countries. Elimination of these vestiges of the old communist mentality will hasten the coming of viable economies and true democracies. Weakness and deprivation result from closed systems as found in communist societies. Strength comes from diversity and openness

All of the former communist countries are struggling through this time of transition. President Vaclav Havel of the Czech Republic related in June, 1998, some of the deficiencies in his country. He could have been speaking for all of the Newly Independent States as he said, "We need more transparent ownership rights, transparent attitudes toward capital markets and economic restructuring even though it means some social risks."[6] Concern and assistance from the developed nations of the world is still important in accomplishing the successful transition.

Notes

1.   The Soros Foundations for an Open Society were created by Mr. George Soros, wealthy financier and philanthropist.   Every newly independent state has Soros Foundation offices where democracy and free market practices are promoted.

2.   James K. McCollum, "Effectiveness of Management Internships: The Romanian Experience," *Proceedings of the American Society of Business and Behavioral Sciences Fifth Annual Meeting*, Las Vegas, February, 1998. This paper describes the information learned at a reunion of the Romanian interns that took place in May, 1997. The former interns were generally faring better than their contemporaries in Romania: setting up new companies and having a better understanding of managing under free market conditions than similarly placed managers.

3.   The letters were published in newspapers in Baia Mare, Cluj, Piatr Neamt, Sibiu, and possibly some other cities. The letters were put on a website in Bucharest. I have received e-mail messages from both Romanians and Americans who have read the letters.

4.   Thomas Carothers of the Carnegie Endowment for International Peace reports that "A bankruptcy law was finally enacted in mid-1995, but the law has few teeth and is unlikely to do much to move the restructuring process forward." Thomas Carothers, "Romania: Projecting the Positive," *Current History* (March, 1996), p. 119.

5. Ibid. "The Romanian state remains a largely unresponsive bureaucracy that acts less like a servant and more like a self-sustaining organism primarily concerned with its own preservation and enrichment," p. 120.

6. David Lynch, "Havel Finds Little Time for Rest, *USA Today*, June 19, 1998, p. A10.

APPENDIX A

EFFECTIVENESS OF MANAGEMENT INTERNSHIPS: THE ROMANIAN EXPERIENCE

James K. McCollum
University of Alabama in Huntsville

An internship has been defined as "One component of a student's educational preparation for a career. It is an outside of class learning situation. The student is placed directly in the field with a veteran practitioner as his mentor. The student is allowed the opportunity to assume responsibility and to function in a 'real life' situation" (Koehler, 1979). The idea of internships for business students evolved from the medical field where the concept developed in first in European medical schools then was transplanted to U.S. medical schools in the late nineteenth century. "An internship is supposed to be an educational experience which prepares men for the practice of medicine...To be practicing physicians, all medical school graduates must serve an internship" (Miller, 1970).

Gradually, the use of internships began to appear in other professions, but without the stringent requirements put on medical interns. Government oriented internships in the federal government were introduced in the 1940's, with many claims of nepotism as legislators saw that their relatives received the benefits of this program to put novices into these training positions. Over time, the government intern programs improved in their image as devices were introduced to limit the effect of politics in the intern selection process. Many states developed intern programs to encourage students to learn more about state government (Koehler, 1979).

The use of internships in business firms in the U.S. has taken on a different direction from that found in the medical or public administration fields. In those professions, interns are supposed to learn what a practitioner does on the job and thus give practical experiences for the budding professional. While this is partly true in business internships, the greater interest is in using the method as a means of recruiting talented business school seniors (Pianko, 1996). In that respect, the internship program is like that in the legal profession where promising third-year legal students are invited to intern in some of the best legal firms.

INTERNSHIPS FOR ROMANIAN BUSINESS PERSONS

With the demise of communism in the former USSR and Eastern European satellites, the U.S. government initiated several programs to help the former socialist countries to learn how to establish free market business practices in their newly freed economies. All of the newly independent states had been under state controlled "command" economies for at least forty years and those of the former Soviet Union, for seventy years. Business persons in those countries had to learn new concepts: supply and demand, efficiency, quality, consumer choices, profitability, etc. They had never had to consider these concepts before because the state made all of the decisions for them concerning what to produce, where to obtain supplies, what level of quality, what to charge, and with how many employees. Profitability was never considered.

After 1989, all of the newly independent states were faced with great problems of transitioning their economies into the free market. Members of the U.S. government saw the need for programs that would quickly get some free market knowledge into the newly independent states. One program that was introduced in 1991 was the Central and Eastern European Training Program (CEETP) of the U.S. Information Agency that was directed at bringing middle-managers in the fields of (1) local government/public administration, (2) independent media development, and (3) business administration to the U.S. for short (four- to ten week) internships (USIA, 1991). It was believed that such internships would indoctrinate a core of practitioners in operating in a free market environment. The program was activated by publishing a request for proposal in the Federal Register to get interested parties to compete for contracts to administer intern programs. The bidders were required to find ongoing working situations in public administration, communications, or business administration where the interns could be placed to receive practical experience.

After having a professor working with Romanian students as a Fulbright professor for eleven months, we decided to use his knowledge of the country and his contacts to establish an intern program for Romanian business persons. Our first attempt to create such a program was successful in obtaining placements for eight interns, but our proposal was not accepted by the U.S. Information Agency. At that time, we turned to a private funding source, the Soros Foundation for a Open Society, to bring five interns to work in businesses in the Huntsville, Alabama area. With the help of the Soros field office in Bucharest, Romania, we identified five interns, three males and two females, and brought them to Huntsville in February, 1994. After a one week orientation with classes and visits to local institutions and businesses, we placed them in three companies for four weeks.

We had instructed the "mentors" in the companies taking interns to rotate the interns through several of their operating sections to see all of the differing operations and to talk with operating managers. Each intern was also required to complete a project established by the mentor which would require the intern to research a business problem and develop some depth of knowledge about the company's activities. Members of the companies reported that they had enjoyed the opportunity to further the intern's knowledge and wanted to continue to communicate with their intern(s). The experience seemed to be very enlightening to the interns and they returned to Romania with our expectations that they would share their new knowledge with others.

With an established "track record," we sent another CEETP proposal to the U.S. Information Agency to bring twenty managers and four business educators in 1995. This time, we received a contract from U.S.I.A. The Soros Foundation was again a partner in the program. In this instance, we had found intern positions for the twenty managers in twelve companies. The business educators interned in our university, with visits to some local businesses.

For this larger program, we had the Soros Foundation in Bucharest advertise for candidates. The initial screening was accomplished by Soros administrators and Romanian educators as they chose fifty candidates to come to a "Free Market Management Workshop" from the large number of applicants. The five day workshop was conducted in Bucharest in December, 1994, by three of our UAH professors. They selected the 24 interns, (equal numbers of males and females and equal numbers from the capital city, Bucharest and from cities outside Bucharest: Timisoara, Brasov, Iasi, Cluj, Baia Mare, and Oradea), to come to Huntsville.

We brought the interns in two groups: twelve in March-April, 1995; twelve in April-May, 1995. Again, we used the pattern of the one week orientation and four weeks in a company. The program seemed to have as much success as before, so we again proposed to have a similar program in 1996. This time, we would have no business educators, only managers. We had Soros advertise in March, 1996, we conducted preliminary screening in April, and we ran the workshop in May. As before, we had equal numbers of males and females, but only eight from Bucharest and sixteen from other cities: Baia Mare, Cluj, Constanta, Craiova, Iasi, Oradea, Sibiu, and Targu Mures.

As before, we brought the 1996 interns in two groups: twelve in September-October, 1996; twelve in October-November, 1996. Using the same pattern with the 1996 interns, we again got very positive responses from the interns and their mentors about the value of the program. At the end of November, 1996, we had trained fifty-three Romanian managers and business educators and we hoped that we had made some impact on the newly independent Romania. Although it may have been premature to see any results from some of these former interns, we decided to have a reunion in 1997 to see how their careers were progressing and to establish a program by which we might track these individuals in the future.

INTERN REUNION IN BUCHAREST

We planned a two day reunion in Bucharest for May 9-10, 1997. Invitations were sent, along with a college newsletter. All former interns were encouraged to contact their former colleagues in the program and make certain everyone knew about the reunion.

Preliminary returns from the interns were encouraging, with more than thirty positive responses. During the two days of the reunion, a total of forty-two former interns attended some of the sessions.

We had prepared a questionnaire to determine how the careers of the interns had progressed since the internship. Completion of the questionnaire was the price of admission to the program which included two lunches and a dinner at the prestigious Cercle Militar. During the program, representatives from U.S.I.A, Soros Foundation, and UAH spoke, then over the two days twenty-four of the former interns spoke about their experiences subsequent to the internship.

The results from the questionnaire and the spoken narratives were very encouraging. Most of the interns said that their careers were going very well, although they were not satisfied with the business environment in Romania. Nineteen interns said they had started new companies and 23 (some of whom had already started businesses) said they were planning to start new businesses. One of the most heartening presentations came from the oldest intern. He had been 51 years old when he was an intern in 1994 and was 53 as he stood before us in 1997. He said that he had taken a leap of faith in leaving his established job and starting a new business in 1996. At the time of the reunion, he was employing two full time employees and 40 part time employees in an architectural business. Another 1994 intern had become a project manager for IBM in Romania. He said that being a project manager in a large company is very difficult, but "Everything I learned in Huntsville was useful." A 1996 intern wanted to start a permanent intern alumni organization and volunteered to create a newsletter for it.

QUESTIONNAIRE RESULTS

We used a questionnaire with several Likert scale answers to determine the progress made by the interns subsequent to their stay in America. In order to determine if progress shown was only resulting from the additional experience managers gain with the passage of time, we used a similar questionnaire on thirty Romanian middle managers who had not gone outside of the country for any kind of internship or management training program. We used the time frame, "since 1994" because that was the year that our first interns had come to Huntsville. Examples of questions used are as

follows"
1. Compared to my work situation ("before the internship in Huntsville" for former interns, or "since 1994" for non-interns) in my current job, I have more responsibility.

1	2	3	4	5
( )strongly agree	( )agree	( )undecided	( )disagree	( )strongly disagree

For this question, the interns' average score was 4.24, while that of non-interns, it was 4.06. This difference was not significant. For subsequent questions, we will eliminate the stem of the question which is common for all and state only the descriptor.

2. ...I have higher status. Interns: 4.15; Non-interns: 3.82.

3. ...I direct the work of more subordinates. Interns: 3.12; Non-interns: 3.05.

4. ...I have more purchasing power from my salary, that is, after taking inflation into account. Interns: 3.57; Non-interns: 3.45.

5. ...I am more capable of managing subordinates. Interns: 4.35; Non-interns 3.18.

6. ...I am more capable of dealing with other managers. Interns 4.41; Non-interns 3.95.

7. ...I am more capable of dealing with outside influences such as government regulation.
Interns: 4.0; Non-interns 3.91.

8. ...I have a better understanding of "free market" practices. Interns: 4.33; Non-interns 3.05.

9. ...I understand management processes in a for-profit business. Interns: 4.42. Non-interns: 2.91.

The raw data shows that the interns had superior scores on all questions and significant differences at the .05 confidence level were found on questions 2, 5, 6, 8, and 9.

Additional information from the interns revealed that 19 had started new businesses since the internship and 23 planned to start new businesses. In the control group, four had started new businesses since 1994 and 10 said they planned to start a new business. These data tend to indicate that the former interns have more confidence in starting new businesses in Romania than do the non-intern managers. One of the objectives of the program for business administration was oriented toward management training and another was toward small business development (USIA, 1994). Thus it would appear that our internship activities in Huntsville had accomplished these objectives.

SUMMARY AND CONCLUSIONS

Internships have been used in the medical profession in the U.S. since the turn of the century. Their use in other professions is more recent. In recent times, they have been used in business training as a method to identify good candidates for businesses to employ. Since the demise of communism in Eastern Europe, internships have also been used by the U.S. government as a method by which Eastern European managers can be trained for managing under free market conditions.

In the years 1994, 1995, and 1996, fifty-three Romanian managers came to the Huntsville, Alabama area to participate in five-week internship training. After their return to Romania, a reunion of the former interns was held in Bucharest with 42 of the former interns attending. In addition to having the interns speak about their experiences, a questionnaire was completed by each former intern to learn more about the effects of the internship. Questionnaires were also completed by a control group of 30 similarly placed managers in Romania shortly after the reunion closed. A comparison of the responses from the former interns and non-interns shows that the former interns say they have more capability to manage under free market conditions than their contemporaries who had not experienced such an internship. Since some of the former interns had returned to Romania seven months prior to the reunion, it can be assumed that the differences between interns and non-interns will increase with time.

REFERENCES

Koehler, C. (1979). *Public Administration and Public Sector Internships: 1960 through 1977.* Monticello, Illinois: Vance Bibliographics.

McCollum, J. (1997). Using the Case Method in a Former Socialist Country. *Interactive Teaching & Learning: Case Method & Other Techniques.* H. Klein, ed. Madison, WI: Omni Press.

Miller, S. (1970). *Prescriptions for Leadership: Training for the Medical Elite.* Chicago: Aldine   Publishing Company.

Pianko, D. (1996). Power Internships. *Management Review* 85, (December), 31-31.

Bibliography

Alexandru, Sorin. "The Challenge of Power," *The Times Literary Supplement*, January 19-25, 1990, pp. 55-56.

Baker, Randall. *Summer in the Balkans: Laughter and Tears After Communism.* West Hartford, CT: Kumarian Press, 1994.

"Belarus: Market to Open Gradually," *Business America*, 114, No 8, April 19, 1993, pp. 27-28.

Behr, Edward. *Kiss the Hand You Cannot Bite: The Rise and Fall of the Ceausescus.* New York: Villard Books, 1991.

Campeanu, Pavel, "The Revolt of the Romanians," *New York Times Magazine*, February 1, 1990, pp. 1-2.

Carothers, Thomas. "Romania: Projecting the Positive," *Current History*, (March, 1996), p. 119.

Clark, Ed and Anna Soulsby, "Transforming Former State Enterprises on the Czech Republic," *Organizational Studies* 16, No. 2, 1995, pp. 215-242.

Codrescu, Andrei. *The Hole in the Flag: A Romanian Exile's's Story of Return and Revolution.* New York: William Morrow and Company, Inc., 1991.

Codrescu, Andrei. *The Life and Times of an Involuntary Genius.* New York: A Venture Book, 1975.

Codrescu, Andrei. *Zombification: Stories from NPR.* New York: Saint
Martin's Press, 1994.

Coffee, John C. Jr. "The Privatization of Eastern Europe," *New York Law Journal* (July 23, 1992), pp. 5-7.

Cornis Pope, Marcel. *The Unfinished Battles: Romanian Postmodernism Before and After 1989.* Iasi, Romania: Polirom Co. S.A., 1996.

Courtois, Stephane. *Le Livre Noir de Communisme: Crimes, Terreur, Repression.* Paris: Centre Nationale de Research Scientifique, 1998.

Dacalu, Adrain. "Romania's Iliescu Calls for Economic Relaunch," *Reuters Money Report* (Lexis-Nexis Service) July 4, 1994.

Daniels, Anthony. *Utopias Elsewhere: Journeys in a Vanishing World North Korea, Cuba, Albania, Romania, Vietnam.* New York: Crown Publishers, Inc., 1991.

Dogaru, Mircea and Mihail Zahariade. *History of the Romanians: From the Origins to the Modern Age.* Constantin Draica, trans. Bucharest: Amco Publishing House, 1996.

Drakulic, Slavenka. *Cafe Europa: Life After Communism.* New York: W.W. Norton and Company, 1997.

Drakulic, Slavenka. *How We Survived Communism and Even Laughed.* New York: W.W. Norton & Company, 1991.

Drakulic Slavenka. *How We Survived Communism and Even Laughed.* New York: Harper Perennial, 1993.

Flagler, Carolyn and Aurelia Nicoara. "Romania: Land of New

Opportunities,"*Contract Management.* June, 1994, 10-18.

Frydman, Roman, Andrzej Rapaczynski, and John S. Earle. "Romania," *The Privatization Process in Central Europe.* London: Central European University Press, 1993, pp. 208-262.

Galbraith, John Kenneth. *The Good Society.* New York: Houghton Mifflin Company, 1995.

Gallagher, Tom. *Romania After Ceausescu: The Politics of Intolerance.* Edinburgh: Edinburgh University Press, 1995.

Georgescu, Vlad. *The Romanians: A History.* Columbus, Ohio: Ohio State University Press, 1991.

Golea, Traian. *Romania: Beyond the Limits of Endurance.* Miami Beach: Romanian Historical Studies, 1988.

Hudelson, Richard H. *The Rise and Fall of Communism.* Boulder, CO: Westview Press, 1993.

Ionescu, Dan. "Romania: The A to Z of the Most Poluted Areas," *Report on Eastern Europe.* May 10, 1991, pp. 20-25.

Kim, Julie and Francis Miko. *Poland, Czech Republic, Sovakia, and Hungary: Recent Developments.* Congressional Research Service of the Library of Congress, 6 January, 1993.

Kohlberg, Laurence. "Stage and Sequence: The Cognitive-Developmental Approach to Socialization," in *Handbook of Socialization Theory and Research,* D.A. Goslin, ed. Chicago: Rand McNally, 1969, pp. 347-380.

Kornai, Janos. *The Road to a Free Economy: Shifting From a Socialist System.* New York: W. W. Norton, 1990.

Lynch, David. "Havel Finds Little Time for Rest," *USA Today,* June 19, 1998, p. A10.

Mackensie, Ross and Todd Culbertson, eds. *Eyewitness: Writings from the Ordeal of Communism.* New York: Freedom House, 1992.

Matley, Ian M. *Romania: A Profile.* New York: Praeger Publishers, 1970.

McCollum, James K. "Astrom United, S.A. Bucharest, Romania," in *Case Studies on Economic Transformations: Russia, Kazakstan, and Eastern Europe,* ed. by Bob Donnorummo. University of Pittsburgh: Center for Russia and East European Studies, 1997, pp. 247-256.

McCollum, James K. "Romania's First Steps Toward Privatization," in *Struggling With the Communist Legacy.* A. Helweg, P. Klein, and B. McCrea, eds. New York: Columbia University Press, 1998.

McCollum, James K., Adriana Coada, and Nicolae Mihaita, "Comparison of Management Styles of a Former Socialist Country to Those of Western European Managers," *Economic Computation and Economic Sybernetics Studies and Research.* Vol. XXIX, 1-4, 1995, 73-78.

National Agency for Privatization. *Privatization Programs in Romania.*

Bucharest: November, 1992.

"Petre Roman Presents Government Programme and New Ministers," BBC Summary of World Broadcasts (Bucharest Home Service, aired on May 25, 1990).

Pachepa. Ion Mihai. *Red Horizons: Chronicles of a Communist Spy Chief.* Washington, D.C. : Regnery Gateway, 1987.

"Pachepa Calls for Dissolution of Political Police," *Ziua.* (April 30, 1997), p. 1

Pakula, Hannah. *The Last Romantic: A Biography of Queen Marie of Roumania.* New York: Simon & Schuster, Inc., 1985.

Posner, Vladimir. *Eyewitness: A Personal Account of the Unraveling of the Soviet Union.* New York: Random House, 1992.

"Postscripts," *Wall Street Journal.* (August 17 and 18, 1997), p. A-9.

"Still on Track: Romania," *The Economist.* 344 (August 232, 1997) pp. 40-42.

Robinson, Anthony, "Survey of Privatization in Eastern Europe, " *Financial Times* (3 July, 1992), p. 3.

Roman, Carol. *Ultimele 100 de Zile Nefaste: Sfiritul Clicii Ceausescu.* Bucharest: Case de Editare "Glob," 1990.

"Romania: Introductory Survey," *The Europa World Yearbook, 1997.* Vol. II. London: Europa Publications Limited, 1997, pp. 2731-2739.

Romanian Development Agency, *Investment Opportunities in Romania,* Bucharest: Tiporex, SRR, 1992.

Romanian Development Agency. *Law Digest for Foreign Investors. February, 1992.*

Schopflin, George. *Politics in Eastern Europe: 1945-1992.* Oxford: Blackwell Publishers, 1993.

Shook, Carrie. "Romania Rising," *Forbes* (September 22, 1997), pp128-131.

Tismaneau, Vladimir. *Reinventing Politics: Eastern Europe from Stalin to Havel.* New York: Free Press, 1992.

Treptow, Kurt W. ed. *A History of Romania* 3d ed. Iasi: The Center for Romanian Studies, 1997.

Verona, Sergiu and Francis T. Miko. *Romania, Bulgaria, Albania: Recent Developments.* Congressional Research Service of the Library of Congress, January 13, 1993.

Weekly Compilation of Presidential Documents 33, No. 29 (July 21, 1997), pp. 1061-1063.

Whitehorse, Mark. "Entrepreneurs Find Belarus is Tough Going," *Wall Street Journal,* (June 1, 1998) p. A14.

INDEX